Preaching
The Miracles

Series III, Cycle B

Harold H. Lentz

CSS Publishing Company, Inc., Lima, Ohio

Copyright © 1999 by
CSS Publishing Company, Inc.
Lima, Ohio

Scripture quotations are from the *New Revised Standard Version of the Bible*, copyright 1989 by the Division of Christian Education of the National Council of the Churches of Christ in the USA. Used by permission.

Library of Congress Cataloging-in-Publication Data

Lentz, Harold H. (Harold Hervert), 1910-
   Preaching the miracles. Series III, Cycle B / Harold H. Lentz.
     p.   cm.
   Includes bibliographical references.
   ISBN 0-7880-1358-0 (pbk. : alk. paper)
   1. Jesus Christ—Miracles. 2. Bible. N.T. Mark—Homiletical use. 3. Lectionary preaching. I. Title.
BT366.L46   1999
226.7'06—dc21
                                        99-36619
                                          CIP

*To our children, Julie and Tom,
and our daughter-in-law, Marty,
whose love and concern for us in our
retirement years have reflected the
Christian spirit of St. Mark.*

Table Of Contents

Introduction   7

Miracle One   13
Healing A Demoniac
Mark 1:21-28
Epiphany 4

Miracle Two   25
Healing Peter's Mother-In-Law
Mark 1:29-31
Epiphany 5

Miracle Three   37
Healing A Leper
Mark 1:40-45
Epiphany 6

Miracle Four   47
Healing A Paralytic
Mark 2:1-12
Epiphany 7

Miracle Five   57
Healing A Withered Hand
Mark 2:23—3:6
Proper 4
Pentecost 2
Ordinary Time 9

Miracle Six   67
Stilling A Storm
Mark 4:35-41
Proper 7
Pentecost 5
Ordinary Time 12

Miracles Seven And Eight   **79**
    Healing An Issue Of Blood
    Healing The Ruler's Daughter
    Mark 5:21-43
    Proper 8
    Pentecost 6
    Ordinary Time 13

Miracle Nine   **91**
    Healing A Deaf-Mute
    Mark 7:31-37
    Proper 18
    Pentecost 16
    Ordinary Time 23

Miracle Ten   **101**
    Healing A Blind Beggar
    Mark 10:46-52
    Proper 25
    Pentecost 23
    Ordinary Time 30

Epilogue   **111**

Bibliography   **115**

Introduction

John Mark, author of the Gospel which bears his name, had two qualities for which we can be grateful. First, he had considerable talent as a writer. Living in a day when very few people were sufficiently educated to be able to write, he was proficient in doing so. Furthermore, he actually liked to write. As a result, we are able to read his inspired Gospel of Jesus Christ. This work is especially noteworthy because it is an accurate biography of our Lord which has come down to us through the ages. Though he never met Christ personally, there are several reasons why he was unusually well-informed about our Lord. It was in his parents' home that members of the early church met to worship and to discuss their faith. One can picture the youthful Mark spending many an hour absorbed in listening to people of deep faith as they talked about the infant church and its founder. He would bear that imprint throughout his entire life. It was to that same home that Peter and Paul went occasionally for Christian fellowship, thus providing young Mark with the opportunity to associate with the two greatest saints of early Christendom. Paul even took John Mark with him on an early missionary journey. Though they had a falling out for a time, Paul called Mark to his side when languishing in a prison in Rome where he met his death. Another sturdy missionary, Barnabas, asked Mark to accompany him when he took the gospel to foreign lands. For both men Mark served as secretary. That meant that in addition to hearing all the discourse about the life and teachings of Christ, Mark would have it imprinted on his mind by being able to reread his writings at will.

A second quality of Mark was his natural attraction to spiritual matters. By his association with Peter, Mark was destined to become greatly inspired about the person and power of Christ. Peter had actually lived with Christ for several years as one of the original twelve apostles. As an eyewitness, he could give firsthand accounts of various events in the life of Christ. Mark enjoyed an extremely close relationship with Peter, serving him also as his secretary and writing down for posterity the statements of the famous apostle. Thus, Peter is to be credited for much of the material in the Gospel of Mark.

Of the four Gospels, Mark's is believed to be the first one that was written. Apparently Matthew and Luke copied extensively from Mark, which explains why they are so similar as to be called the Synoptic Gospels. If the three are placed side-by-side for comparison, it is easily noted that they cover the same material, follow much the same order, and frequently use similar words and expressions. It appears that the other writers had Mark's work in hand and made much use of it.

The date of the writing of Mark's Gospel account is not known with certainty, but it is generally believed to be around 65 A.D. That was a time when the Christian believers were undergoing fierce persecution, many of them dying by cruel torture. Mark's Gospel portrays a Christ in whom his followers could unhesitatingly place their trust. They could die as martyrs and be resurrected as saints. To that end, he made it clear that Christ was the Messiah whose coming had been foretold in the ancient scriptures. He describes many miracles as proof that Christ was not mere man, but had supernatural power as the Son of God. That relationship with God enabled him to restore sight to the blind, to walk on water, and even to control the forces of nature. Most of all it gave him power to raise the dead, and even for himself to return from the dead and to continue to dwell among the living. Mark wanted to tell of the miracles in order to persuade his readers that Christ was indeed the long-awaited Messiah in whom they could fully place their trust.

Mark had one purpose in writing which was particularly relevant to the Jews. He hoped to persuade them that Christ fulfilled all their own religious prophecies concerning the coming of the Lord. At the same time he hoped to make clear the differences between Christianity and the religion from which it sprang. In this way he is a bridge between the Old and the New Testaments. He makes it clear that Jesus did not come as a conqueror in THIS world. His calling was not to lead a mighty army of the type so familiar to the people living in those Roman times. Rather, he appeared as the ruler of another realm, one which called for repentance, and proclaimed the good news of a spiritual kingdom which was eternal. Mark explains how the Son of God could accept humiliation and, with it, the terrible suffering, disgrace, and even death upon a cross. Such suffering and humiliation of God is a concept Jews have always found to be unacceptable.

Just as the date of the writing of this Gospel is unknown, so also is the place where it was composed. Here circumstantial evidence must prevail. The likeliest place is Rome, for it was believed that Mark, who joined Paul there during Paul's last days on earth, wrote this Gospel while he was with the Jewish Missionary to the Gentiles. There may have been others who wrote about the life of Christ before Mark did, but of the works that have come down to us through time, his is the earliest. It is well to remember, as stated earlier, that this was a time of monstrous persecution for the fledgling church under the tyrant, Nero. And, as has been noted, Mark wrote in part to encourage Christians to be faithful during such troublesome times. The death of his personal friend and teacher, Paul, would have had a profound effect on Mark. His readers were to think deeply about Christ and the hope of eternal life which Christ had nourished while on earth.

Perhaps we ought to ask, just what is a miracle? It can be described as an event in which God's power enters into a human situation of life on earth. This explanation assumes that one first accepts the reality of God, in order to believe in the miracles of Christ, God's Son. If there is an all-powerful God he can certainly perform miracles. And if he is a God of love he will surely hear his people when they cry out to him in prayer. Thus, the miracles encourage us to come to Christ.

It was obviously a joy for Mark to tell of the miracles because he believed in them. The whole question of miracles is subject to different interpretations by various individuals. Some people flatly deny the validity of miracles and try to explain them away on the basis of human interpretations. However, their explanations raise many questions which, in turn, are difficult to accept. And yet these same doubters are willing to confess to miracles taking place all around them. They call it a miracle when someone walks away unscathed from a terrible automobile wreck. They freely call it a miracle when someone recovers from the grip of a deadly illness.

In our interpretation of the miracles we need to remember one thing well: do not push them too far. It is the same with the parables of Christ. There is a central point, or two or three, and then we must conclude our interpretation. By pressing too far, one can read into the account things that are not really there, that were not intended to be derived from the incident. It is when we go too far that doubts concerning our own interpretation arise. Along this path we can deceive even ourselves.

The accounts of the miracles make an appeal to a broad diversity of readers. They are able to arouse interest in a wide array of individuals. The stories of Christ healing the sick and infirm strike a sympathetic chord with many who are suffering from poor health or other afflictions. Reading about a woman who was too bashful to confront Jesus face to face, and only touched the hem of his garment when she was in a crowd surrounding him, is encouraging to many who are by nature shy and retiring. Miracles involving fishing have their special following. Christ's power and authority over wind and waves find sympathetic listeners in sailors. Thus the Sailors' Hymn directs our thoughts toward the "Eternal Father, strong to save, whose arm doth bind the restless wave."

Christ did not perform the miracles for personal gain. He was never paid anything for performing them. He received no appointments to high office because of them. His miracles were performed to draw people to God and to place their faith and trust in him. At the same time they met various human needs, revealing God's personal awareness of what happens on earth, and showing his overarching love for everyone. God's mercy is for all who come to him in faith.

These miracles can have a profound effect on those who hear of them. They are powerful teachings of great spiritual truths.

One final question about the miracles will conclude this introduction to the wonders performed in Christ's day, and immediately thereafter. The question is: When did the day of biblical wonders end? Or did it?

There is no definite answer. As has been stated previously, while Christ was on earth, and shortly thereafter, he and his apostles performed miracles for two reasons. One was to reveal his power as the Messiah, the Son of God, so that people might believe in him. The other reason was to make believers of many people and thus establish the young Christian church as it struggled against almost overwhelming odds, including persecution and death.

Apparently the apostles carried on the work of miracles to a somewhat diminishing extent. It is believed that this was due to the fact that the infant church had now developed to a point where it no longer needed miracles to survive, and the divinity of Christ, in whose name the miracles were performed, was widely accepted among the believers.

Since Bible times, miracles have assumed a different form. It is true that one branch of the church has occasionally indulged in accepting and teaching some legendary miracles, but Protestants argue about many weaknesses in such teachings. There have also been many claims by so-called faith healers, alleging themselves to be miracle workers, whose claims have been proven to be false — but not before many gullible people have been badly deceived.

Post-Bible miracles usually have certain characteristics in common. Often they are not instantaneous, but consume some time before coming to reality. Secondly, they are often the apparent result of group prayer. Someone is in danger of dying from an accident or illness, so a prayer circle forms to offer up petitions to God for the victim's recovery.

For a person to be canonized in the Roman Church there must be proof of the person's having performed at least one miracle, or for miracles to have been performed by calling on his or her name. In the case of the latter, they are after-death experiences. To some, this practice seems to redirect the result of prayer from God to the one proposed for sainthood. The requirement of a miracle can be waived by the Pope.

The miracles of Jesus, as recorded in Mark's Gospel, are in a class by themselves. Performed by none other than Christ, the Son of God, they have been an inspiration for countless missions of devout believers across the centuries.

11

Miracle One

Healing A Demoniac

They went to Capernaum; and when the sabbath came, he entered the synagogue and taught. They were astounded at his teaching, for he taught them as one having authority, and not as the scribes. Just then there was in their synagogue a man with an unclean spirit, and he cried out, "What have you to do with us, Jesus of Nazareth? Have you come to destroy us? I know who you are, the Holy One of God." But Jesus rebuked him, saying, "Be silent, and come out of him!" And the unclean spirit, convulsing him and crying with a loud voice, came out of him. They were all amazed, and they kept on asking one another, "What is this? A new teaching — with authority! He commands even the unclean spirits, and they obey him." At once his fame began to spread throughout the surrounding region of Galilee.

Background Material

It was the Sabbath and, following his habit, Jesus was in the synagogue for worship. Even to this day, it is a part of Sabbath worship in the synagogue for someone to read the day's lesson as the basis for the day's study and possible discussion. The reading is from the Pentateuch, the first five books of the Old Testament, which is the official Jewish version of the Holy Scriptures. It is housed in an Ark which is the central focal point of the congregation. The words of the Pentateuch are written on a parchment which is rolled around two scrolls. The parchment can be rolled forward or backward to the desired reading.

While the local rabbi is often the one who reads the lessons, visitors are sometimes honored with this exercise. As Jesus became better known he would be asked to read the scripture lesson and elucidate upon it. On this occasion, Jesus was standing before the congregation, beginning his exposition. The worshipers were amazed at his informed wisdom and knowledge of the Pentateuch and at his ability to hold the attention of the audience with his message. Apparently he was an excellent speaker and a stark contrast to the dull scribes who usually droned on about the demands of the law.

But on this day he was rudely interrupted while delivering his message. A man who was afflicted with what was supposed to be demons entered the synagogue. Almost immediately the demon let out a loud shriek, which must have startled the congregation. But Jesus was unperturbed. He took command of the situation by ordering the demon to leave the man. The congregation, already astonished at Jesus' ability to teach so well, was now absolutely amazed that he could cure the "incurable."

Demons
Belief in demons is of ancient origin. In the very early books of the Jewish scriptures the idea was widely presented as fact. Rather logically, they were believed to be the evil spirits emanating from Satan, just as the angels were good spirits who spent their time serving God. While they roamed everywhere, it was believed that cemeteries were their central dwelling places. Among the rituals of the ancient Jewish church were rites for exorcising demons.

Early Hebrews probably inherited their belief in demons from their Semitic ancestors. Also, their contact with the Babylonians and Persians would bring this influence to them. The polytheism that was widespread at that time was fertile ground for adoption of the belief that demons held power over human beings. So the Jews of that day believed, without reservation, that human beings could be possessed by demons.

The rite of exorcism is still practiced in our day, though very seldom. There is a church ritual for it among both Jews and Christians. However, in this account by Mark, Jesus did not use any special rite. It was by a simple command from him that the possessed man was freed of his terrible addiction.

As has been stated, in Christ's day, there was universal belief in demons. In many areas of human ailments, where ignorance prevailed, demons were given the blame. There was a demon for every illness. One can understand why. Illness was certainly not good, but could be branded as evil, and demons supposedly caused the evil that roamed the earth. Because of the crudeness of medical knowledge at that time, a hole was often bored in the skull of one so possessed, in the belief that this would permit the demon to escape.

There is much to be pondered in the truth that Jesus possesses power over all negative things. Many clinical psychologists have eliminated the spiritual dimension in their attempts to heal, even deriding the idea that faith can play an important part in healing. But currently the tide is turning. A growing number of clinical psychologists believe that the use of spiritual resources can be a tremendous boon in the cure of depression, anxieties, the fear of death, and the fear of the future. This is the cause for the spread of holistic medicine.

Church Attendance

Jesus set us a good example by faithfully going to the synagogue to worship on the Jewish Sabbath. It was the custom at such services to enroll the Torah and read an appointed lesson for that day. Whenever there was a distinguished visitor present, he was asked to speak on the scripture lesson. Usually such lectures could be dull and boring, emphasizing the many demands of the Law of Moses. One can imagine how refreshing it must have been to listen to Jesus when he told of the Spirit behind the Laws and explained the Law's true meaning. The apostles also preached in the synagogue on many occasions, especially Paul, whose reputation as a stalwart Christian eventually led to his rejection as a preacher in the synagogue.

On this particular Sabbath, while Jesus was standing before the worshipers in the synagogue, a man entered who had a severe affliction which people ascribed to his being possessed by demons. The demoniac could enter the synagogue because of an open-door policy which permitted anyone to attend. His presence is a symbol

15

of how good and evil are associated in this world. Sums of money, amassed by people with the good intentions of helping charitable causes, are bilked by an evil treasurer overcome with greed. In many forms trust is betrayed when evil appears among the just and good. Even religious leaders go bad. Sin penetrates everywhere. Some people are cured through faith and prayer, while others of a similar spirit die from the same illness in spite of prayer. Within each person both good and evil reside, warring against each other. Thus we speak about bringing out the good or the best in someone.

In this miracle the evil demons are meeting the sinless Christ. At his word the demons, who shrieked when they came near to the Savior, were expelled and left the man whom they had tormented for so long. This miracle revealed the wide scope of Christ's power. He has dominion over all things, the evil world where Satan reigns, as well as the spiritual realm. He has power over all that is seen and unseen.

Sermon Material

What Have We To Do With You?
Temptations have existed since the time of the first man. Today they seem to be more widespread than ever. Depending on the area where they apply, they carry certain names such as white-collar crime, street crime, and so forth. With so many forms of temptation before us, it will help clear our judgment if, when tempted, we ask, "What does this proposed action have to do with Christ and his spirit?"

1. With the temptation to adultery or unfaithfulness in marriage.
2. With the temptation to pilfer.
3. With the temptation to cheat on your tax returns.
4. With the temptation to continue a bad habit.
5. With joining in association with the wrong people.
6. With taking an action against someone.
7. How relevant is Christ to life in today's world?
8. What does Christ have to do with YOU?
9. How much authority does Christ have in people's lives today?

Amazement

When Christ first spoke in the temple the people were amazed. Even more so were they when he worked a miracle. His "congregation" thought they knew this young man, but were not aware of his ability as a public speaker. But he revealed in his presentation something much greater than a talent for speaking. He exhibited a profound knowledge of the scriptures, of theology, and of human nature. He was not at all cowed by his audience, but spoke as one with authority. They did not realize at that time how great was the authority with which he spoke to them.

How much more stupefied they must have been when he nonchalantly performed a miracle before their very eyes in the synagogue. They were utterly amazed at what they had seen take place. A man they all knew to be badly demented, whose irrational ways they ascribed to the work of demons, was actually cured by a word from Jesus.

We too should be amazed by Christ as more and more we learn of him and his mighty deeds. Without the element of amazement our spiritual life can become very commonplace. It is meant to be exciting. Why should we not be constantly amazed by the thought that Almighty God is with us in our personal lives? He actually loves us, each one of us, as his child. That is a startling fact, for he is Lord of the universe and is its creator. We should be deeply impressed also by his daily provisions for us, by his glorious promise that we, too, shall conquer death, a blessing almost unbelievable. "What a great God" should constantly be the expression of our hearts as we contemplate his goodness to us both in time and in eternity.

Amazement can have a further beneficial effect. It can make us want to know more and more about Christ, about his fascinating life while on earth, and the many wondrous deeds he performed. Amazement can well be a part of everyone's religious experience. It gives our beliefs a lift of spirit. It helps us to realize how truly great God is, and the enormous force of his power. It keeps fresh in our minds the glory and the reality of God's magnificent plan of salvation, assuring everyone of eternal life made possible through

Christ's death on the cross, through whom we can anticipate a glorious resurrection to a life far above comparison with our present one.

Recognition Rather Than Amazement

There is a lesson here for everyone. We must see the potential among the young people in our midst. The temple worshipers thought of Christ only in terms of a carpenter's son, whom many had observed working in his father's shop. Nothing unusual here! Just so, some very normal young person in our circles of family, neighborhood, or church may have the potential of becoming another Thomas Edison, Florence Nightingale, or even a president of the United States. We dare not downplay the talents of those with whom we are familiar, but must encourage them to do their best to attain a high level of achievement in life.

Astounded At His Teaching

Have we not experienced the difference in gaining and holding our attention between two speakers, when one appears to be expressing original thoughts and the other to be only quoting what he has read, or else citing as authority someone other than himself? The scribes were of the second kind, while Christ gave refreshing new insights into the application of the Law. This astounded the people who knew his background and his youthful past. Their astonishment led them to go about describing what they had seen transpire in word and act; and in their telling, the news about Christ was spread far and wide.

Illustrations

"They Were All Amazed"

A graduate student at Yale University was given the assignment to go to Sterling Library and to its guarded rare book room to read an original publication of one of Martin Luther's original tracts. The student's first reaction to the assignment was one of disgust.

He asked himself why go to the trouble of laboring through a difficult first edition when an easy-to-read modern translation was available? Not only was the original in German, but it was written in the German style of nearly five centuries ago, which was considerably different from the modern German learned in the classroom. But in carrying out the assignment the student came to realize why it had been given to him. Not only was it an unusual thrill to hold in hand an original manuscript of such age, but the strong imprint it made on the early reader was apparent. Centuries ago an earlier reader had read that tract when its ideas were completely new and was visibly impressed by its revelations. That reader could not help but write on its margins such words as "Imagine that!" "Think of it!" The impact which that tract had made was a thrilling revelation to the student.

The Bible is an amazing revelation of matters such as life after death. Do we let its contents fill us with awe and utter amazement as we contemplate its mighty truths? We ought to be astonished at what we learn from the scriptures, and never be led to say with a yawn, "So what!" The words of Christ should not produce this reaction, nor should they ever be considered dull or boring.

* * *

A young grandmother told her granddaughter that the two of them would get up early the next morning to see something surprising. So the next day, in the very early hours before dawn, the two of them sat on a doorstep facing east. Then the grandmother told the child to watch the eastern horizon. Soon a red curve of light appeared. As they watched, the curve kept widening. Sitting in awe, the little girl witnessed her first brilliant sunrise, when the sun has an enormous size and rises slowly as a huge ball of fire. The little girl asked in a hushed whisper, "Does that happen every day?" Have we let life become so dull and introspective that we no longer look with amazement at the wonders of nature: a sunrise, or the rising of a full moon, or the multicolored sky during a sunset? Life is full of God's creations which should amaze us. A very partial list should include the changing seasons, the warm friendships of life, and our ability to live out our days without crippling illness.

"What Have We To Do With You?"

This statement can be taken as a cynical expression. It is in a league with the following sentiments: "Mind your own business." "Stay out of our way; we have nothing in common." "Go back to your own place and to your assigned business."

There are many selfish people in this world who have such an attitude about Christ. They want him out of their way, to be able to exploit people without a condemning conscience. They know he represents another way of life entirely, and they do not want to be reminded about their shortcomings. So they want to be left alone. If the scriptures show them to be wrong, they simply alter the words to their own advantage. What has Christ to do with it is the question facing the slave trader, the vice king, the drug lord. It is the question thrust at each one of us whenever we are tempted to do evil. But some sneeringly ask, "Don't I have the right to live my own life as I please?" in spite of the harm it will do to others.

Jesus answers this question with the words: "Come out of him." He would tell us to come out of it, to get our thinking straight. He says it to those who want to exploit their fellow man, be it with child pornography or some crooked scheme which appeals to those who want to get rich quickly.

Church Attendance

The Battle of Gettysburg, during the Civil War, is a subject of much ongoing discussion. The defeat of the Confederate Army has been blamed in part on the actions of General J. E. B. Stuart. A couple of days before the decisive battle, he departed on what turned out to be a useless raid. In so doing, he is said to have lost contact with the main army. Because of this, he could not inform General Lee what he had learned about the plans of the Union Army.

Losing contact with the main army was a serious error. It is equally culpable in any conflict. This includes the warfare in which Christians are continually engaged against evil. The main army is the vast numbers of Christian believers who gather regularly for Sunday worship. Such blessings as spiritual renewal, a clearer understanding of biblical truths, and an increased loyalty to Christ are among the helps that derive from fellowship with other Christians in worship services.

* * *

This miracle took place in a synagogue, or church. That was the place to find Christ on the Sabbath. That is where the demoniac was cured. Do we excuse ourselves from regular Sunday worship services, acting as faultfinders or showing indifference, or do we attend church regularly?

The story is told that Queen Elizabeth I attended a service in her chapel and sent a critical word to the organist declaring that the organ was out of tune. The organist, a Dr. Tye, courageously replied that it was not the organ but the queen's ears that were out of tune.

Do we stay away from church, even criticizing it? It could well be we who are at fault, not the worship service. It is sobering to recall that when *Tannhauser* was first presented in Paris the audience hissed in criticism. Now we judge the opera to be great, but a proper appreciation of its grandeur was lacking in the audience who rejected it.

Our souls were created to be recipients, and then donators, of God's love. It is at church that we meet Christ, hear his gospel, and have our souls tuned to God.

Sunday Observance

It is important to observe Sunday as a day of rest. Some time ago a study was made of the machinery in a manufacturing plant. One line of machines was kept running seven days a week, with no letup. The other line was idled on each Sunday, during which time it cooled off and was left untouched. The machines which were idled each Sunday needed fewer repairs than the others. Even iron and steel can fare better when rested at times.

But the mere form of going to church, important as that is, is not enough. The purpose of going to church is to grow in faith and in commitment to God. One needs repeated reminders of the requirement to love our neighbor, to be a forgiving person, just as God forgives us. We must not be misled with our church attendance; attending church is imperative.

The Voice Of Evil

During an argument, if a person does not have a good answer, he turns to anger, or to false reasoning, perhaps doubletalk. In a way that is true of this demon. Before Christ had said a word, he called out a question which was irrational. In asking "What do you have to do with me?" he was trying to turn the tables by implying that Christ should stay out of it. That is the way the voice of evil speaks.

One of the best known of advertising logos has been the picture of a dog listening to a victrola, with the words underneath: "His master's voice." It is to emphasize the clarity of the recording, as the dog recognizes the voice that the old-fashioned victrola is reproducing. One of the ills of society today is the inability of many people to recognize the false voice of evil.

In every generation evil has its voice. In the case of the demon there is the implication, impudently stated, that Christ should mind his own business. And there is the further implication that Jesus and the demon have nothing in common. And indeed they do not. Today those who would attack evil and its vociferous claims are charged by the voice of evil with being old-fashioned, of being out of date, as they seemingly oppose the virtue of freedom of speech. We hear the voice of evil in all the forms of pornography as they seek to lure us to buy their wares. Their appeal creeps into all facets of modern life. Over the years the voice of evil has defended slavery, excused child labor, and defended many of society's ills. When we hear that voice we must recognize it as the voice of the demon who confronted Christ. "What have I to do with you?" insinuates that evil has the right to its own life, unfettered by Christian morals or the laws of society. Christianity opposes this view and presents Christ as the Lord of life who brings blessings to those who hear his voice and obey him.

Who Is This?

This is the way those who witnessed the miracle expressed their amazement. This is a question that confronts anyone who would be a Christian. Is Christ the Son of God? Is he the Savior of the world? Is he all-powerful, all-knowing? To answer such a question properly from the heart is life's greatest boon. It is like a question on an exam which everyone must take. We answer it satisfactorily or we fail. It is a personal question, asked directly of you.

Miracle Two

Healing Peter's Mother-In-Law

As soon as they left the synagogue, they entered the house of Simon and Andrew, with James and John. Now Simon's mother-in-law was in bed with a fever, and they told him about her at once. He came and took her by the hand and lifted her up. Then the fever left her, and she began to serve them.

Background Material

Situated very close to the synagogue was the house where Peter lived when in Capernaum. It must have been practically next door, for the scriptures say that "as soon as they left the synagogue they entered into the house of Simon."

It was noontime and the handful of disciples were expecting to enjoy a midday meal together. But Peter's mother-in-law, their intended hostess, apparently noted for her cooking, had developed a high fever and had taken to her bed. Eager to entertain Peter's friends, especially the one who was being proclaimed as the Son of God, one can imagine her frustration and disappointment when this illness struck her.

Earlier this morning in the synagogue, Christ had healed a badly troubled man, thus emphasizing his right to heal on the Sabbath. Now for a second time he was asked to do so. He was following his belief that the Sabbath was made for man, and not man for the Sabbath.

When asked to minister to Peter's mother-in-law, Jesus could rightly have said: "Let me rest for a while, for I am tired after leading the morning worship, with the challenge of the demons who were controlling an unfortunate man." But he did not. Instead he immediately faced another problem, near at hand in that household, and he performed a healing.

It was a wordless miracle. Nothing was spoken between the two, according to the account. Taking the woman's hand, he raised her from her bed. Instantly she was healed and able to assume her duties in serving the meal. Her first desire was to return to normal activities.

With this miracle, Jesus continued to astonish his followers as he demonstrated his Godly powers. This particular miracle was probably the least impressive of the many Christ performed. It was hardly to be ranked in importance with curing someone afflicted with the dread leprosy, or raising someone from the dead. But it does take its place in rounding out the account of the many types of miracles performed by our Lord during his earthly ministry. The variety of the miracles showed the breadth of Christ's dominion: over nature when stilling the tempest, over all manner of diseases, even over death.

Was the purpose of this particular healing so that the men could have their expected dinner served to them? Hardly. They were all concerned for the suffering woman and were driven by their Christian concern for others. Believing in Christ's power, "they told him about her at once."

They were concerned for a family member. Families are supportive. This one cared about one of its own. So they sought to help her in her distress. How wonderful when families are bound together with a sense of unity.

Peter's House

In 1988 archaeologists unearthed what they are convinced are the remains of Peter's house in Capernaum. The site is right, near the location of the synagogue. In the ruins of the house many artifacts have been discovered to substantiate the claim that this was indeed Peter's house, where Christ performed the miracle of healing Peter's mother-in-law. The artifacts include some fishing hooks and a picture of a boat, so that it appears to have been the house of a fisherman of long ago. There are crosses sketched on some of the walls, designating the occupant as an early Christian. Other artifacts connect this house with Peter, and the claim has been substantiated by scholars.

Marriage Of Clergy

In reporting about Peter's mother-in-law, the scriptures are at variance with the teaching banning marriage of clergy. Specifically, if Peter is to be called the first Pope, then it would seem that his example of marriage would be followed by his successors, as indeed it was for many centuries. The Pope whose decree banned priestly marriages was Hildebrand, known as Pope Gregory VII. He issued the decree near the end of the eleventh century. This can be considered rather recent in the long history of the Christian Church. There was a good, though self-serving, motive behind this decree. It was meant to free priests from family obligations so they could give all their time, effort, and devotion to the church.

But there are many other facets to the issue, such as the difficult denial of human sexual needs and the protection of priests from charges of sexual promiscuity. Further, the ban on clergy marriage has resulted in heavy losses among the ranks of the clergy. This has assumed alarming proportions in recent years. Many priests have left the Roman Church to marry. Seminary enrollment has been decimated by the rule that many young men are not willing to accept. As a result, numerous Roman Catholic parishes in the United States and elsewhere are facing a serious shortage of essential clergy. In some parishes, a priest must serve two or more congregations. The Papacy, however, has adamantly refused to rescind the edict, choosing to defend the ban on priestly marriage.

Sermon Material

From Church To Home

Jesus carried his divine power from the synagogue to Peter's house where he healed Peter's mother-in-law. Like Jesus, we make our way from our house of worship back to our residence. How far does the inspiration of the service carry with us? How soon do we lay aside the inspiration of Sunday and return to involvement in the many claims of the mundane life? The influence of the worship service is meant to apply to our daily interests and efforts. The power of God, proclaimed in church, can be a power we do not lose, but one that pervades our daily life of prayer and good works. It is something to be retained in our hearts as a source of inspiration and a guide for daily living. What a shame to leave behind, at the church door, the influence of the worship service.

Christ In The Home

What a blessing it is to the occupants when Christ enters a home! There are so many ways in which his presence can be made known and felt within the family circle. One excellent way is by establishing daily devotions. Worship is not to be confined to the sanctuary. When family members unite in prayer and the reading of scripture, there are marvelous results in the spiritual life and growth of the family. Religious pictures and other wall decorations do a great deal to develop the Christian atmosphere of a home. They serve as constant reminders to the occupants of their spiritual needs. But best of all is to let the spirit of Christ rule the actions within the walls of one's residence. Family discussions can help direct one's thoughts to ways of helping others in school, at work, and at play, thus encouraging a desire to be of service. It is so easy to edge Christ out of family relationships, but it is also a simple matter to let him rule in the interactions of family relationships.

Conversely to the blessings of Christ's influence in the home, how easy it is to forget him, and for all to become involved in each one's personal interests and pursuits. Christ can be squeezed out so easily that we do not even sense his absence. How tragic that was in the life of Samson, recorded in the Old Testament. Samson was so blessed, but by his neglect he lost contact with God. It happened so gradually and silently that "he did not know that the Lord had departed from him."

If we welcome him, Christ will meet all of a family's deepest needs. He can put an end to strife, eliminate the separation of divorce, do away with physical abuse, and instill an atmosphere of peace and love. He will replace despair with hope, develop family unity, and give life the lift that is falsely promised by alcohol and other drugs. He can soothe our fears, allay our anxieties, and strengthen our desire to resist temptation.

Healing On The Sabbath

This healing took place on the Sabbath. The Sabbath, or Sunday, is supposed to be a day of rest. But it is also intended as a day of healing — healing of body and of soul. This basic purpose of the day seems to be lost in today's emphasis on materialism. "Business as usual" on Sunday simply indicates a grasping for more money and the accumulation of financial success. Just as there is desperate need for the body to rest each night, and thus be restored for the activities of another day, so one day in seven is required by the demands of the body for rest and relaxation in order to be prepared for another workweek of labor and stress.

When properly observed, Sunday can restore health to both body and soul. Sunday is really supposed to be such a day of healing. In the attitude and actions involved in neglecting God, as witnessed in today's society, there is an ever-widening gulf between God and his creatures. But this rift is bridgeable if we turn to making proper use of the benefits offered by a sincere observance of the seventh day, a day of rest, worship, and healing.

Trust Your Problems To God

Ordinarily the apostles might not have known what to do when they were expecting to enjoy a dinner, only to find that their hostess was incapacitated. But they turned the problem over to Christ, who quickly solved their dilemma by healing the woman. Because they trusted Christ to have the right answer, the scriptures inform us that "they told him immediately."

We can always trust Christ with our concerns. His deep love for us was amply demonstrated by his death on the cross, where he freely gave his life in our stead. Now he encourages us to bring our burdens to him. Remember his encouraging words: "Come unto me ... and I will give you rest."

Do we think first of turning to Christ when any trouble or a crisis arises? Do we call upon him, trusting that his help is available?

Why isolate yourself from the greatest possible source of help? Remember the words of the hymn: "Take it to the Lord in prayer."

Importance Of The Homemaker

It appears that it was necessary for the mother-in-law to be healed if the dinner was to be served. Because she could return to her duties, the household and their guests were able to enjoy their Sabbath meal. Too often the importance of the woman in the home is overlooked. It is really she who holds the family together, looking after the needs within the family shelter. Usually it is she who has the task of planning the meals, accumulating the items of food, and then preparing the meal. She looks after the cleanliness of the home and the health of the family members. She must budget her time and money and the investment of her services. The present-day movement for the liberation of women dare not overlook her importance to the home, the rearing of the children, and the companionship of her husband. If she is thoughtful, she will realize that in her tasks she has a calling from God, the same as a call to the ministry or any other respected profession.

A Limited Audience

Some of Christ's miracles were performed before large audiences, as in the feeding of the 5,000. As a result, large numbers believed in Christ, for they had witnessed his superb power. This miracle was performed within the privacy of a home, with only a few people present. But the result was the same. Those who witnessed it were profoundly impressed. And the report of what had transpired was spread by word of mouth with the speed with which such news can travel. Here is where personal evangelism can play so large a part. We are to be witnesses for Christ. It is through us that word must spread of the marvelous works of Christ and of his power and authority as the Son of God.

Seeking The Help Of Christ

"Take it to the Lord in prayer" is the advice of a time-honored hymn of the church. The handful of disciples who were with Jesus on this occasion were quick to tell him of the distressing fever. On other occasions they brought their discussions and questions to him for his help.

Do we take advantage of this source of help? What an opportunity prayer offers us to seek the wisdom and help of Christ in all dilemmas. Another hymn proclaims that "Jesus loves to answer prayer." With such help readily available, how foolish it is to try to solve our problems alone. How often we fret and worry needlessly, when the thing troubling us can be put into his hands.

Christ Brings Us Strength And Inspiration
To Solve Our Problems
1. Christ animated the widow with the necessary strength to perform her tasks.
2. Christ can give us the strength to continue ministering in his name.
3. We should, as Christ's people, apply this strength.

Never Tire Of Doing Good
1. We are tempted to stop giving to so many worthy appeals.
2. We are tempted to stop giving so much time in service to others.
3. We want to be freed from meeting the needs of elderly parents or others.
4. We want to excuse ourselves from such tasks in order to think of self.
5. But the scriptures tell us never to tire of doing good; Christ did not.

Christ Went Apart To Pray
1. The power of prayer to restore.
2. The need to pray for guidance.
3. The need for prayer in all phases of daily life.

Illustrations

Look Upward

"When the outlook isn't good, try the uplook." This verse appeared on the outdoor bulletin board of a church. It reminds the passersby that Christians have another dimension in their lives. They can look up to God for help and cheer.

We are told that one of the tasks in training a guide dog for the blind is to get the animal to raise its sights. It must look out not only for objects that would be an obstruction at a dog's height, but must learn to consider the height of the person it is guiding. For instance, some protruding object sticking out from a building at a height of four to six feet is nothing to block the path of a dog, which can simply walk under it. So he must be made alert to look higher than himself in order to protect the blind person he is leading. Man is described as an upward-standing person. He is capable also of lifting up his eyes unto the hills, of looking to Almighty God for guidance through life.

Serving Others

The world took note when Mother Teresa died. To the very end of her long life she spent her entire energy on helping others. Most of her efforts were directed toward helping the "poorest of the poor" in the slums of Calcutta, India. For this, she won the praise and adulation of people of all religious faiths, and even of those who proclaimed themselves nonbelievers. She was acting out her faith. Christ would impel all his followers to forget themselves and bury their life in loving labors for others. Christ declared that even he came into the world not to be ministered to, but to minister to others.

Church Charities

Churches are not given enough credit or recognition for the immense amount of social welfare they perform. The total Sunday offering of the churches in the United States comes to nearly fifty billion dollars per year. We are told that nearly half of this huge sum is invested in institutions of mercy such as hospitals, orphanages, homes for the aged and the like, as well as programs to serve the poor and needy. The latter includes such things as food banks, food kitchens, disaster relief, distribution of free Bibles, used clothing distribution, as well as prison visits. The list is endless. Churches are not supposed to be clannish, but are expected to give of themselves and their means, unselfishly, to aid a world in need.

Unenforceable Obligations

"And she began to serve them." She did not need to do so. She had been sick in bed and could easily have chosen to rest a while before rising. Her daughter could possibly have substituted for her, or even Peter himself, for it was his home. But without the obligation to do so, she carried out an unenforceable obligation. She voluntarily took up the duties of serving.

It is reported that she got off her sickbed healed of her illness, and immediately turned to the task of serving dinner to Christ and his followers. How can we serve Christ today? We can do so by helping others.

There are some things demanded by law, which, if not met, are punishable by fines or imprisonment. But there are other things which might be called obligations which are not enforceable and must be done voluntarily or not at all. One can offer his services to help a person in need or willingly meet some obligation even though he cannot be forced by law to do so. One cannot be forced to love his neighbor, for instance, or visit the sick and lonely. But one can willingly fulfill the obligation to do good even though such obligations are not enforceable.

A striking illustration is that of a General Gourrand, whose arm was badly damaged by shrapnel. He was told that the arm could be satisfactorily restored if he remained in the hospital for a year to undergo a series of surgeries. When told this, he asked how long he would have to remain in the hospital if the arm were amputated. The verdict was four months. Whereupon he immediately stated curtly, "Cut it off." He did what no one could have demanded of him, and after four months was back with his troops. Such willing sacrifice is the way a committed Christian meets his unenforceable obligations.

Serving Christ

A retired gentleman, who wanted to feel useful as a Christian, developed the routine of helping to feed the poor. He would go to a local bakery where they sold day-old bread at greatly reduced prices. There he would purchase so many loaves that they filled his car trunk and the back seat of his automobile. Then he would drive into a poor section of his city and give out the loaves of bread to anyone who came to him. On the days that he appeared, the word quickly spread throughout the area that he was there with free bread. He came to be known as "the bread man."

Another example is that of the Christian dentist who sympathized with those who needed dental care but could not afford his services. So he opened a Saturday office in a poor section of his city where he practiced dentistry free of charge one morning per week. There is no doubt that he did much good and his efforts were greatly appreciated.

Still another example is that of a woman of frugal habits who regularly saved her small weekly surplus, which she took to the bank. At her death her will directed that the entire bank account was to go to Carthage College to pay for the tuition of those who did not have the means of attending college. To the surprise of many, the estate amounted to almost 800,000 dollars.

There are countless ways in which all of us can be servants of the Lord, simply by helping the poor and needy. Christ said that by doing this to one of his we are doing it to him.

Family Unity

As soon as the disciples entered Peter's house they took Jesus to the bedroom, where Peter's mother-in-law lay ill, in order that Christ might minister to her. This was a display of family unity, of care and concern shown for one another. In a sense, we are all part of a greater family, the human race. It should be a cause for deep concern for us when we see a fellow human being in great need. Unfortunately this is not the case in many instances.

Recently in a California city, a cab driver was in a parking lot when he was confronted by four men. People looking out the windows of a nearby apartment watched as the four men mercilessly beat the cab driver, continuing to do so until he collapsed and died. They continued to watch as the four took the body of the dead man and stuffed it into the trunk of his cab. While there were numerous witnesses, no one called the police. Their only excuse was that they knew gangs were operating in the area and they feared retribution if they became involved. How widespread is this attitude? Where is society headed if we do not care about one another?

House Calls

Christ came into Peter's house. He brought his healing power which resulted in an immediate cure for Peter's mother-in-law. Today doctors no longer make house calls and it is necessary to go to their offices to secure their help. But Jesus continues to enter into the homes of his followers. He wants to be invited so that he can influence all members of our family. He offers such blessings as faith, hope, the assurance of eternal life, and the awareness of his constant guidance as we face the challenges of life.

What Happened To Your Hand?

According to the account of this miracle, Jesus offered his hand to Peter's mother-in-law. She took it and, when lifted to her feet, was healed. She was able to return to her duties in preparing and serving a Sabbath meal. How often the hand of Christ is extended to us. We can respond and be helped, or we can reject it and suffer the great loss of his blessing. After all, it was Christ's hand that would be pierced by a spike, as our Lord was nailed to the cross on which he died for our sins.

There is an impressive painting which pictures Christ surrounded by a group of little children. They seem to be very happy in the presence of our Lord, their little faces wreathed in smiles. But little children are curious and they do not hesitate to ask questions. One child is fascinated by the wound in Christ's hand. The painting is given the title of her question: "What happened to your hand?" It was a hand wounded for us and still bearing its awful scar. It has been said that nails could not have held Christ on the cross if his love for us had not done so. The hand of Christ reminds us of God's love. It reaches out to us today in every time of need, offering us help and forgiveness. What is our reaction?

Miracle Three

Healing A Leper

A leper came to him begging him, and kneeling he said to him, "If you choose, you can make me clean." Moved by pity, Jesus stretched out his hand and touched him, and said to him, "I do choose. Be made clean!" Immediately the leprosy left him, and he was made clean. After sternly warning him he sent him away at once, saying to him, "See that you say nothing to anyone; but go, show yourself to the priest, and offer for your cleansing what Moses commanded, as a testimony to them." But he went out and began to proclaim it freely, and to spread the word, so that Jesus could no longer go into a town openly, but stayed out in the country; and people came to him from every quarter.

Background Material

There is considerable variety to the miracles performed by Christ. One was performed in a synagogue (curing the demoniac), another in a home (healing Peter's mother-in-law), and this one he performed on a public thoroughfare. While Jesus and his disciples were walking, a man afflicted with the terrible disease of leprosy approached them. Fear of leprosy was so great that strict laws had been passed concerning the actions of one so afflicted. The law demanded that lepers should isolate themselves from society, and keep themselves some distance from other people lest they contaminate them. A leper was called upon to shout out "unclean" when approaching others, to warn them to keep their distance. A leper was to come no closer than six feet to anyone. But this man desperately sought a cure and had faith that Christ could bring this to pass. So he came up to Christ, humbly kneeling before the Lord as a gesture of great respect. His confidence, or faith, in Christ is evident when he says: "You can heal me if you choose." He had broken the rule about non-approach. Jesus, taking pity on the man and wishing to reward his faith, touched the man. This act of touching a leper meant breaking another man-made rule. And to the wonder of all those present, Christ's touch brought instant healing to the pitiful leper. It was an amazing miracle, revealing Christ's power as the Son of God. Christ is still the great healer to whom we may turn for cleansing from sin and evil.

Next Jesus issued a stern command to the healed man. He was to follow the prescribed method for being declared one who was healed. He was to go to the priest and fulfill the prescribed rites. Perhaps Jesus issued this order to make sure the man was accepted back into society.

Secondly, Jesus sternly commanded the man not to tell others about his healing. This seems strange, but Christ had a purpose in his directive. But the healed leper was so overcome with joy and relief that he could not contain himself. He went about everywhere, reporting to all who would listen that Christ had healed him of the dreaded disease. Jesus had given the command of silence because he wanted people to come to him for spiritual ministry, and not to witness a miracle worker. Performing magic was a far cry from Christ's call for repentance and his offer of God's grace. He was teaching about faith in God's plan of redemption through Christ's sacrifice on a cross.

Because of the man's persistent witnessing, large crowds formed to see the man who had cured an incurable disease. To avoid the large assembly of people, Christ went to the countryside, seeking privacy. But in huge numbers the crowds sought him out even there.

The validity of the report of this miracle taking place receives its credence from the fact that it was witnessed by a group of people, and by the resultant rush of people who wanted to see the miracle worker. They brought their own sick and lame to Christ to receive his healing powers.

By our own faithful witnessing for Christ we can help build the kingdom of God on earth. The challenge before every Christian congregation is for its members to tell the unchurched about the wondrous works of God. The result will be a rush of people who want to hear more.

The Disease Of Leprosy

Today, cancer seems to be one of the most feared of all ills that can be inflicted upon us. It is so silent that often the first one hears about it is when the awful words of possible doom are pronounced: "You have about six months to live."

In Christ's day the horror of horrors was leprosy. It continued to strike terror into human hearts across the centuries until fairly recent times. Finally a cure was discovered which is effective in most cases.

Because it was so terrible, leprosy totally isolated the one afflicted from all of society. The leper was to live apart and forego all human relationships. The disease was terribly mutilating. Fingers and toes could rot and drop off. The face could become grotesque with the loss of a nose. Its awful effects have been aptly described by William Barkley in his book, *The Gospel of Mark*:

> *It begins with pain in the joints. Then there opens on the body patches (discolorations). On them, little nodules form. The skin is thickened. The nodules gather especially in the folds of the cheek, the neck, the lips, and the forehead. The whole appearance of the face is changed till the man loses his human appearance. The nodules grow larger and larger. They ulcerate and from them comes ... a discharge. The eyebrows fall out, the eyes become staring, the voice becomes hoarse and the breath wheezes because of the alteration of the vocal cords. Slowly the sufferer becomes a mass of ulcerated growths. The average course of the disease is nine years and it ends in mental decay, coma, and ultimately death. The sufferer becomes utterly repugnant both to himself and to others.*

There is no doubt that it is a living hell, and it had to be endured while separated from the support of family, friends, and society in general.

What Power Jesus Possessed To Overcome So Terrible A Tragedy

People avoided the leper, fearing for their very lives if it should contaminate them. But Jesus did not. He approached the man and did the unthinkable: he touched him. The man with the dreaded leprosy was healed because Christ shut the door to no one. It was he who said: "Come unto me, ALL ye ..." He also declared: "He who comes to me I will in no way turn out." Christ's welcome to the leper reminds us that we may all be welcomed by him. No sin is so great as to separate us from God's love. Jesus is the bridge to our Father's forgiveness. But we can block out Jesus from our lives, to our own severe loss. What unnecessary weight we carry when we do not turn to God in any time of trouble. After all, he is waiting with open arms to receive us, and to grant us help, and rest, and the wondrous provision of his grace.

What power Christ revealed in performing this miracle. What authority he demonstrated. We are reminded of the soldier at the foot of the cross who, having witnessed the death of Christ, declared, "Truly this was the Son of God."

Sermon Material

This Miracle Is Applicable To Everyone

This man had leprosy and we do not. So how does the miracle apply to us? In this instance leprosy can be understood to mean any form of disease; when properly understood, this places each of us in the shoes of the leper. Even though we do not have leprosy, the miracle is not irrelevant to us. Today we still have seemingly unconquerable health problems. Cancer can strike anyone; and only a percentage of cancer victims are able to achieve recovery. AIDS is another form of modern-day "leprosy." It is spreading fast and is a threat to everyone. In such instances we are dependent upon Christ to answer our pleas for help, and to receive his mercy. The answer is not always what we wish, but the opportunity to be in touch with Christ is available.

We need to remember Christ's power to heal. Even turning to him as a last resort can produce many benefits. There are faith healings today that baffle doctors and lay people. Without the desired cure, it is beneficial to have the blessings available through contact with Almighty God. And the age of miracles is not over, as many can attest.

"Tell No One"

As stated in the introduction to this book, Christ did not want his basic message to be diluted. He had come to call people to repentance and to live according to God's will. He realized that the widespread telling of his cures would bring multitudes to him who would come out of curiosity and without regard for his basic message of salvation from sin.

Christ Touched Him

The leper was supposed to stay at least six feet away from everyone, and to touch him was unthinkable. But Christ let him draw near and actually reached out his hand to touch him. And the touch of Christ healed.

There are many ways in which Christ can touch our lives, and always with positive results. We can make contact with him through prayer, by reading the Bible diligently, and in worship in his sanctuary or in private; and always the result is a genuine blessing.

Christ can touch our self-centeredness, leading us to think of others and even to associate with the unfortunate. Without Christ's influence, our first reaction to such people can well be to turn away, not even to see them sometimes, as though they did not exist, and quickly to reject their call for help. But when Christ touches us, we respond affirmatively to such needs.

That same touch or influence can strengthen our resolve to resist whatever temptations assail us to live for ourselves alone, strengthening our resolve to live instead as one of God's concerned people.

Christ's touch can change a personality. It can make us meet life bravely, freeing us from fear of unacceptance, anxiety about what tomorrow might bring, and even fear of death. Through him we can become fearless, happy individuals who meet life's challenges with courage and a smile.

The Need For Faith

Having heard about the miracles which Christ was performing, this leper knew that Christ could heal him. However, he was not certain that Christ would do so. After all, he had been cast out of society. When Jesus said to the leper, "I am willing," he spoke words of encouragement to us. We need to remember God's promise to us that he will never leave us nor forsake us. How reassuring are the words in Psalm 50:15 where God assures us: "Call upon me in the day of trouble; I will deliver you." Faith plays an important part in our relationship to God.

The Value Of Reverence

The leper fell on his face before Jesus. It was an extreme act of reverence. Reverence has its rewards. Unfortunately it has largely disappeared in today's society. God's name is often taken in vain. Those in authority are demeaned. It seems that only the Boy Scouts with their statement that "a Scout is reverent" are left to support this worthwhile attitude.

Christian Service

We are by nature selfish. "What's in it for me?" is an oft-repeated question. It is well said that self-preservation is the first law of life. One accomplishment of the Christian life is to draw people out of their natural self-centeredness and induce them to perform acts of mercy for others. In this, the model is Christ, who said that even he came not to be ministered to, but to minister, and to give himself as a ransom for many.

In the instance of this miracle, Christ went against the self-protective attitude of society in his day. Remember, a leper was considered to be beyond human sympathy. But Christ went against the grain, not hesitating to touch the leper, and so to heal him. Christ's pity was in stark contrast to the condemnation of society.

Should we not follow Christ's example today? There is a crying need for pity and understanding for those whom the world would reject. An advertisement once headlined the words: "There are no bad children." It aimed to turn criticism from the action which was unjustifiable, and replace it with consideration of the child who deserved our love. This sort of mind-set evolves from Christian love. We learn to love the unlovable. This is the motivation for congregations to feed the hungry, clothe the needy, reach out to society's unfortunate, and in so doing break down the false barriers of color, religion, and sex.

Forgivable Disobedience

Civil disobedience was the rage a few years ago. It taught that if a law was thought to be unjust, it was permissible for a person to disregard it. Right, or justice, was given priority over legislative bungling. Moral righteousness was placed ahead of flawed justice. In this miracle, the leper disobeyed the command to keep his distance from other people. He brushed aside this law and approached Christ reverently. Kneeling before the Lord, he pleaded for a cure. But in this instance, he was in contact with the Son of God, the ruler of the universe. The man-made command was disobeyed, but a higher authority brushed it aside, and a pitiful leper was healed.

Recounting God's Blessings

We take so much for granted. We accept so much kindness and consideration without a thought of expressing gratitude. Here the cured leper could not be silenced. He went about vigorously proclaiming Christ's goodness in healing him. As a result, throngs of people went in search of Christ. The hymn calls us to "Count your many blessings and it will surprise you what the Lord has done." Our undeserved blessings include sunrises and sunsets. Night skies are an inspiration when filled with stars or a full moon. There is our health, the food we eat each day, our nights of rest, our friends, such assets as clothing, shelter, a job, education, and a host of other things. How can senseless people think of these blessings unless we remind them? As recipients of all these good things, let them know about the Creator who provides them. Do we speak out? How much gratitude do we express?

Illustrations

Leprosy Of Another Kind

While we do not live in fear of leprosy today, leprosy of another kind is always waiting to infect us. There is a spiritual leprosy which eats away at the human soul, just as the leprosy of Christ's day ate away the human flesh of its victims.

Some years ago a book was written with the title *The Hollow Man*. How hollow, indeed, is that human body which has no inner soul to respond to God! Spirituality is a basic instinct of a human being, and without it we are not complete. We are like hollow men and women.

Love Can Heal

Researchers working with Alzheimer's disease have discovered something which pleases but perplexes them. Sometimes a patient suffering from this disease for which there is no known cure would experience a definite slowing of its progress. Looking more closely, they discovered that such patients were the recipients of much tender, loving care. Some member of the family or a good friend had kept them reassured that they were deeply loved. Love does wonders to the human *persona* and in some cases can be a powerful healing factor. This is especially true of those suffering from depression or sorrow or a keen disappointment.

Christians Can Be Healers

We marvel at the way Christ healed all manner of diseases. But doctors go about doing the same every day. An elderly doctor, nearing retirement, was standing outside a church one day when another man came along. They shook hands and then the newcomer, turning to another man nearby, declared, "This man saved my life. I would not be living today if it were not for him."

How good that doctor must have felt to hear such a testimony about his skills. He had saved a human life. But think for a moment. Christ said that we, his followers, would also do great things. Can not all of us practice the healing power of Christianity? If we make the most of our opportunities, we can all be one to whom others owe their very life, or least a tremendous improvement in it. Our powers of healing include the reconciliation of differences, bringing back together people whose friendships have been broken. We can heal the brokenhearted and the bereaved with our words of Christian comfort and words of hope. We can dispel loneliness by a cheerful visit. There are so many ways in which we, as followers of Christ, the great Healer, can use his teachings to heal people in our day.

We, Too, Need A Cure

There was once a university professor who startled his class by asserting, "I don't need Christ. I have never broken the Ten Commandments. I refuse to be classified as a sinner." Without knowing it he was echoing the sentiment of a rich young ruler whom Christ described. Not faced with leprosy, this miracle may seem unrelated to us. But a little thought makes it clear that we, too, must turn to Christ for a cure. If we are truthful, we will admit that in various ways we have sinned. In fact, we are born into sin. Like the man whom Christ healed of leprosy, we do not need money to be granted an effective cure of our sins. In fact, if we had all the money in the world, we could not buy forgiveness. It is the free gift of God through Christ, the Savior of the world. We must first come to Christ and ask for forgiveness, and he will give us his assurance that we are right with God. Then in gratitude for the forgiveness we have received, we must strive to live the life that is pleasing to God.

"Jesus Could No Longer Openly Enter Town"

Jesus could not enter the town because his presence drew massive crowds who formed to see the miracle worker. This was contrary to Christ's efforts to preach repentance and build a spiritual kingdom. Today there are other so-called reasons for keeping Christ "out of town." Perhaps the biggest opposition to Christ here in America comes from an organization which supposedly advances civil liberty. Instead, it tries to block many of the ways in which Christ's teachings are offered for the benefit of humankind. Prayer, they say, should not be offered at any public school functions such as commencement or in a classroom. A teacher of English must not have a Bible on her desk. The Ten Commandments are not to be displayed publicly, such as on the wall of a school hallway or courthouse. The Christmas creche must not be allowed on any public property. Wherever their efforts are successful, they thus manage to eliminate Christ with his teachings and influence. How much impairment of Christian character and morals results from this offensive, one can only guess. But serious crime has reportedly been rising among young people at an alarming rate. Where are today's youth going to have the distinction between right and wrong effectively emphasized? We dare not confuse the establishment of a religion, forbidden by the Constitution, with the teaching of morals to our youth.

Our Leprosy

Two characteristics of leprosy are the way it spreads over the body and also contaminates other people and, secondly, how it causes death. It is a deadly disease.

A young woman was talented and beautiful. Among other activities, she was a soloist in her church choir. But another member of the congregation became insanely jealous of her acclaim. So she began to invent stories about the soloist and spread unfounded charges of immorality. Other members of the congregation believed her lies. They joined in a spreading ostracism of the young lady, who could not understand the growing resentment against her. She started to feel cut off from others and a keen sense of loneliness engulfed her. When she learned of the false rumors, she did her best to refute them, but without success. The burden of animosity finally became so great that she committed suicide. At her funeral the pastor, who knew the true story, strongly rebuked his parishioners. In his funeral prayer he prayed: "Lord, you have sent me to minister to your sheep. But these are not sheep, Lord, they are ravenous wolves."

We must take care that we do not indulge in the leprosy of rumormongering. We can be either angels of mercy or angels of death. The many forms of leprosy of the soul must be resisted until we are healed by the grace of God.

Miracle Four

Healing A Paralytic

When he returned to Capernaum after some days, it was reported that he was at home. So many gathered around that there was no longer room for them, not even in front of the door; and he was speaking the word to them. Then some people came, bringing to him a paralyzed man, carried by four of them. And when they could not bring him to Jesus because of the crowd, they removed the roof above him; and after having dug through it, they let down the mat on which the paralytic lay. When Jesus saw their faith, he said to the paralytic, "Son, your sins are forgiven." Now some of the scribes were sitting there, questioning in their hearts, "Why does this fellow speak in this way? It is blasphemy! Who can forgive sins but God alone?" At once Jesus perceived in his spirit that they were discussing these questions among themselves; and he said to them, "Why do you raise such questions in your hearts? Which is easier, to say to the paralytic, 'Your sins are forgiven,' or to say, 'Stand up and take your mat and walk'? But so that you may know that the Son of Man has authority on earth to forgive sins" — he said to the paralytic — "I say to you, stand up, take your mat and go to your home." And he stood up, and immediately took the mat and went out before all of them; so that they were all amazed and glorified God, saying, "We have never seen anything like this!"

Background Material

When Christ began his ministry of preaching and healing, his fame spread, until he was well known throughout a large area. He intended to make clear the message of repentance and salvation from sin, but the news of his astounding miracles was something people immediately grasped, and they spread the information everywhere. As a result, throngs sought Jesus in order to have him cure the victims of ill health within their family circle. To avoid huge crowds, Jesus would sometimes go out into the wilderness, but even there masses of people followed.

In this miracle, Jesus had returned to Capernaum, and it was not long before news spread about his being there preaching. Quickly so great a mass of people assembled that the house where he was conducting a service was jammed, while an overflow surrounded the house. This created a problem for a quartet of men who were carrying a badly crippled friend, expecting to put him down before Christ in the hope of a cure. But those who bore the pallet were not to be thwarted by the crowd. They possessed two qualities: persistence and ingenuity.

The houses of that day were one-story buildings with a flat roof. There would be stairs on the outside of the house, leading to the roof. This made it possible for the inhabitants to escape the heat of the house on a warm summer night and to enjoy the night breezes as they slept on the roof. The presence of a stairway outside the house would lead the bearers to think about another way to enter the building. They began to consider reaching Christ by another way since crowds of people blocked the ordinary entrance.

One might still wonder how entry could be gained through the roof. But in that day houses were constructed differently. Modern roofing material was unknown. A roof would be constructed by laying tree branches side by side and in crisscross arrangement. Soft clay was spread over this network and in the hot sun it dried to become almost like tile, and water could not seep through. The four men would have little difficulty in tearing through such construction and creating a hole large enough to lower a pallet.

Jesus must have been startled, but he was deeply impressed by the faith that was involved in this act. First, the paralytic wanted to be brought to Jesus because he believed that Christ could heal him. Secondly, the four men who brought him were persistent in their efforts because they had the same faith. Seeing such strong faith, Jesus applied his power of healing by saying to the paralytic, "Your sins are forgiven." Perhaps it seems strange to us today to hear Jesus say this as a cure for the unfortunate man. But to the people of Christ's day there was a direct connection between sin and sickness. If someone was suffering, it was believed that he must have sinned. Even the disciples once asked Jesus, concerning a man blind from his birth whom they met along the way, whether it was the sin of this man or the sin of his father that had caused the blindness. Jesus answered that in this case the blindness was not the result of sin. Sin can sometimes cause illness, as in the case of syphilis or gonorrhea. With AIDS it can be either the result of sin or come about through impure blood transfusions or needle injections where the victim is innocent of any wrongdoing. One dare not generalize about such afflictions.

In this instance, the man could have felt that sin had caused his problem. He needed reassurance that his problem had been dealt with. His need was to be reassured by Christ that his problem had been properly treated. How wonderful it is for all of us to be assured by Christ, the Son of God, that we have nothing to fear, for God forgives the penitent one. All can be made well again, for Christ is God's answer to sin.

When Jesus healed this man there was great praise from many voices. But not all who were present were pleased. Sitting in the front row where they could carefully watch whatever happened, and hear whatever was spoken, were a few scribes. Scribes were a group of highly educated secretaries to the religious leaders. As such, they were well-versed in Jewish law. Their chief occupation was to serve Jewish law and keep alive its traditions. They were considered people of importance and were even given seats in the Sanhedrin, whose religious decisions carried great weight. The scribes who witnessed the miracle immediately turned on Christ, criticizing his statement to the paralytic, "Your sins are forgiven." They said among themselves that this was blasphemy, for only God could forgive sins. Their statement carried its own explanation. Only God can forgive sins, and since Jesus was God he could do so. He had come into the world as divine Savior, to pay the penalty for our sins, and to offer salvation to all who would place their trust in him.

The scripture passage closes with a description of the effect the miracle had on the throng of people who filled the house. It says, "They were all amazed, and glorified God." Do we do the same, glorifying God for all his mighty works and for all the blessings he lavishes upon us?

Sermon Material

Bringing Others To Christ

The paralytic was fortunate to have such good friends. They were willing to go to all ends in order to see that their friend might be healed. Not only did they carry him some distance, they had the ingenuity and persistence to overcome the obstacle of a crowd which filled the house where Christ was. So when there was a barrier between them and the Lord they overcame it. As a result, their friend DID reach Christ and he received the wonderful blessing of a cure.

Christ has blessings to bestow on anyone who comes to him. Unfortunately, many people need some encouragement, even prodding, to decide to meet the Master. Some may not even know of the blessings he would be glad to bestow. Those who know of Christ and his wonderful gifts need to tell others. They need to be good enough friends to pave the way for their friends to meet Christ. That is a gift all of us can bestow on others. We can prove our friendship by seeing that they know about our Lord, and extend a cordial invitation in his name. Asking someone to join us in church, where we meet the Lord, is an easy and wonderful way to prove the depth of our caring friendship.

The Omniscience Of Christ

Christ is God, and all the attributes of God are his as well. Among them are omniscience, omnipotence, and omnipresence. The scribes did not confront Jesus with their criticism and their belief that he had committed blasphemy. No words were spoken. But Jesus "perceived in his spirit" their critical attitude and he confronted them with it. We worship an all-knowing Christ. He knows our every thought. We can hide nothing from him. This brings added importance to what we harbor in our mind. It leads us to ask, "Am

I filling my mind with things that are acceptable to Christ?" Someone once said, "It doesn't matter so much what I think, but what I think of what I think." This gives us a good standard of measurement, because modern advertising can fill our minds with a wide variety of material; we must judge what is worthy.

Forgiveness Of Sins

The scribes, in their criticism of Jesus, declared that God alone can forgive sins. That is true. When we are guilty of maltreatment of another, we can ask for their forgiveness, and it is in their power to grant or to withhold it. But sin is the term reserved for wrongs against God, and he alone can grant forgiveness. He has provided us with mercy and forgiveness through Christ who came as Savior of the world. He is God. Perhaps it is confusing to some parishioners who hear their pastor declare in a Sunday morning worship service that their sins are forgiven. The key word is "declare." The pastor is not forgiving sins when he says this, but he is declaring that in Christ we are granted such forgiveness.

Prejudice

Much of the world's social trouble is caused by the evil of prejudice. The word "prejudice" means to prejudge, to form judgment before the facts are in. It leads some people to lump together all people of a certain type as objects of scorn. All those of a certain religion or nationality or color of skin are cast aside. The fact that some individuals are worthy of respect for their individual attainment is completely overlooked. The weakness is conveyed in the phrase, "I've made up my mind; don't confuse me with the facts." As a result, hatred and renunciation of others, along with a desire actually to do them harm when possible, rise in the heart of the prejudiced one.

The scribes were unmoved by Christ's miracles. They were out to catch him doing something for which they could condemn him. It mattered not to them that his miracles revealed his divine Sonship. They were out to get him, and everything that stood in the way of this attitude was to be ignored. Jesus once told the story of

Dives and Lazarus, which concluded with a statement concerning those who rejected the Lord. Christ says that such people would not change their minds even if confronted by someone who had risen from the dead. Prejudice must be avoided at all costs. The Christian spirit is one of love for all, and a realization of the worth of everyone.

Criticism

It is so easy to criticize. Before we heap scorn on the scribes for their criticism of the good Christ was doing, we need to look at ourselves. Occasionally, criticism is worthwhile, even necessary to correct a fault. But often it is the product of self-pride, of a desire to tear someone down because we are jealous; or we criticize simply to build on our own ego, believing ourselves capable of judging. But criticism must be handled carefully. Otherwise we can unintentionally become critics of the acts of God. Be careful in criticizing the church, or its pastors, or its people. They are trying to fulfill God's will. They need support and encouragement, not the superfluous judgment of "Monday morning quarterbacks."

Illustrations

Prejudice Following Compassion

In some ways we have made progress in overcoming prejudice toward the homeless. This is indicated in the desire to take pity on the unfortunate. The wandering tramp, or hobo, has practically disappeared from our daily experience, and only older people remember them. They would appear at the back door of homes with a polite request for something to eat. Sometimes they were immediately turned away by those who feared them. After all, they were strangers, and they were unkempt. But sometimes pity for them would stir in the heart of a housewife and she would give them food. But sometimes this act of kindness was followed by what, today, seems like a strange action. When the hobo finished and the plate or coffee cup was returned, the housewife would go to the sink and break the utensils, tossing them into the trash. No one in the family should use that which he had used. Washing in soapy, hot water was not enough. He had left some form of contamination. Such reaction was the result of deep-seated prejudice. The prejudice was stronger than the desire to help an unfortunate human being.

Prejudice Backfires

A prejudiced, high-society woman was planning a garden party in her impressive yard. She was pleasantly surprised on the evening before the big party by a telephone call from her only son, a soldier serving overseas. For some reason she had not heard from him for some time, and was highly pleased to know that he was in New York on his way home. She told him excitedly about the big garden party she was giving, and said she was glad that he would be home to enjoy it.

Then the son informed her that he had an army buddy with him whom he would like to bring along. But this buddy had been badly wounded in fighting for his country. He had lost a leg, an arm, and was badly disfigured from the loss of an eye. When asked whether it would be all right to bring this wounded soldier along, the mother was dismayed. She told her son that the wounded soldier could be a damper on the party, and it would be best if he were not there.

The next day the mother received a notice from the War Department, informing her that her son had committed suicide the evening before. He had been easily identified by his war wounds. He had suffered the amputation of a leg, an arm, and had lost an eye. The pitiful young man had simply wanted to find out if his family would accept him in this condition.

Persistence Pays

The men carrying their sick friend did not let the crowd which blocked their way deter them from getting their friend to Christ. Persistence of this sort is a well-known custom in the East. If a favor cannot be obtained in any other way, then the person or persons seeking it will set to crying and making a disturbing noise around the person whose attention they are seeking. It is hoped that this will catch the ear of the one whose favor is sought, or even wear down his opposition. Thus it is common practice for such a means to be employed by farmers who want their taxes lowered after a year of failed crops. The same means is used when they wish to appeal against the actions of a tyrannical governor. It is said that crowds will gather outside the Shah's palace and there set up a continual howling. They refuse to be silent, or to leave when threatened by guards, until they have had the opportunity to air their grievances. They are known even to surround the Shah's car when he is out driving. Often it works, for the Shah will grant their request, not from his love of justice, but because he wishes to be freed of their annoyance.

Truly Wanting Christ's Blessings

Perhaps it was the cripple himself who urged his friends on, or maybe it was the friends who possessed the indomitable will to see that their friend reached Christ. Our Lord taught that we must have a strong desire, an overwhelming urge, to receive his blessings or we will probably become disheartened and fail to receive what he offers. Christ told of a woman who wanted a judge to hear her plea. But he refused. Instead of giving up she kept repeating her request until the judge was worn out with her pestering and so listened to her case. Another time he told of a man who would not get out of bed late at night to give his neighbor a loaf of bread with which to entertain an unexpected visitor. But the man finally relented and did get up in order to stop the neighbor's persistent pleading.

From the life of Buddha there is the story about a man who came to the great religious leader to obtain a blessing. Buddha asked the man to step down with him into a nearby stream. When they were in the water Buddha suddenly grasped the man and pushed him under the water. In spite of his struggles Buddha kept him beneath the surface. Finally, as he was about to drown he was released and came up, sputtering for air. Then Buddha asked him, "When you thought you were drowning, what was it that you wanted

54

far more than anything else?" "Air," the man replied. Then Buddha said, "When you want a spiritual blessing as much as you wanted air, you will receive it."

"Your Sins Are Forgiven"

As a young pastor I was concerned for the owner of a small hotel who was a member of my congregation but who never came to church. One day I dared to confront him. His story to my query about his lack of church attendance was rather basic. He said that when he was confirmed he learned that it is not what we do that saves us unto eternal life. Salvation is a free gift of Christ who died for our sins. He said that since he was already saved he did not feel the need to go to church. He thought he had understood the Protestant doctrine of justification by faith. But he was only partly right. There is a second part to the doctrine. He was overlooking this part. When we are justified by Christ's death we are no longer driven by the impossible demands of the law to live perfect lives in obedience to that law. But we are now impelled by gratitude to God for his gift of salvation to strive to please him in every way possible. Legal demands have been replaced by loving obedience.

Caring For Others

The story of four men bringing their paralyzed friend to Jesus in the hope of a healing should serve as an example for Christians. We are admonished by Christ to care for our fellow human beings. Fortunate are those who receive help from people moved to charity because of Christian impulse.

Among the works of Thomas Carlyle is the story of a widow. She lived in Edinburgh with her three children who were dependent upon her for their support. When she fell ill with typhus she made a desperate appeal to her community. She said that she was dying and in much need of help. In her plea she said, "I am your sister; one God made us. You must help me." But they rejected her call for help and refused to think of her as their sister. Carlyle states that before she died she infected seventeen others with the terrible typhus. He states that she thus proved that she was, indeed, their sister, whom they should have rallied to help.

All of us share a common bond. We are all part of humanity, and no one lives apart from all the others in our human race. How much it behooves us, therefore, in the spirit of Christ, to help our fellow human beings whenever a great need arises.

Caring About Others

The miracle about the man healed because others brought him to Christ is an example of how we should be concerned about the needs of others and what we can do to help. Perhaps we shrug off many opportunities for doing good by not realizing what we can do, or thinking that our little bit will not help very much.

Such was not the case of the poor working girl who firmly believed in God. She had to work seven days each week and therefore could not volunteer for service anywhere, or even attend church on Sunday. Someone pitied her for her lack of any opportunity to do good. But she surprised them. She said that each day she took the newspaper and prayed for people mentioned there. She said she read the column on birth announcements and prayed that each baby would live a good Christian life. She would read the obituary column and pray for God to comfort the bereaved. She read the wedding announcements and prayed that each couple would enjoy many years of happy married life. She shows us how anyone has the opportunity to be supportive and helpful if we care to do so. Don't forget that selfishness must be thrown off and the welfare of others must play a large part in our life.

Miracle Five

Healing A Withered Hand

One sabbath he was going through the grainfields; and as they made their way his disciples began to pluck heads of grain. The Pharisees said to him, "Look, why are they doing what is not lawful on the sabbath?" And he said to them, "Have you never read what David did when he and his companions were hungry and in need of food? He entered the house of God, when Abiathar was high priest, and ate the bread of the Presence, which is not lawful for any but the priests to eat, and he gave some to his companions." Then he said to them, "The sabbath was made for humankind, and not humankind for the sabbath; so the Son of Man is lord even of the sabbath."

Again he entered the synagogue, and a man was there who had a withered hand. They watched him to see whether he would cure him on the sabbath, so that they might accuse him. And he said to the man who had the withered hand, "Come forward." Then he said to them, "Is it lawful to do good or to do harm on the sabbath, to save life or to kill?" But they were silent. He looked around at them with anger; he was grieved at their hardness of heart and said to the man, "Stretch out your hand." He stretched it out, and his hand was restored. The Pharisees went out and immediately conspired with the Herodians against him, how to destroy him.

Background Material

Jesus and his disciples traveled about on foot. They would naturally take advantage of shortcuts. So this day they walked across some farmland that had been planted with wheat. As they were hungry, they reached out and plucked some of the kernels of wheat to satisfy their hunger. But they were seen doing so by some of

Jesus' critics who immediately called him to account. But as they were stout defenders of the law, and of the scriptures, Jesus answered them out of their own religious writings. He showed them how the law of necessity overcomes, at times, the strict observance of the law. He reminded them how the beloved King David was hungry and entered the holy place in the temple where only priests were allowed to go, and ate the holy bread and gave it to his hungry men. He followed this reminder with the famous maxim: "The sabbath was made for humankind and not humankind for the sabbath."

Mark now adds another act of Christ which emphasizes this thought. He tells of Christ entering a synagogue and in the group of worshipers was a man with a withered hand. Jesus saw an opportunity to teach about Sabbath observance, as well as another opportunity to defy the legalistic Pharisees. So he called the man forward. He asked the man to stretch forth his withered hand, and when the man did so the hand was healed. The amazing thing about this miracle, which distinguishes it from other miracles, was that no request for healing had been made. The man did not approach Jesus with a request for healing. But Christ saw him among the worshipers and recognized his infirmity, a useless hand. It is comforting to realize that Jesus notices things. He is aware of what is going on everywhere, including our daily life.

We are told that this man was a stonemason, a work that required the use of both of his hands. Therefore, the fact that something caused his hand to wither, or shrink, meant he had lost the ability to work at his profession or at most other jobs, for that matter. So Jesus called him forward. Then Christ addressed those who were present, asking them a question. "Is it lawful to do good on the Sabbath day, or to do evil? To save a life or to kill it?" Then Christ asked the man to stretch out his hand, and as he did so it was healed. The man obeyed Christ's command. As a result, the miracle took place.

Jesus excused his Sabbath activity by pointing out how practical his hearers were in meeting the requirements of Sabbath observance. They would make an exception, for instance, if one of their cows fell into a pit on the Sabbath; they would rescue the unfortunate animal. So, to do a kind act of any sort on the Sabbath was not to be condemned. The intent of the day was to bless humankind. It was to serve to bring one closer to God as a day of worship, and help one by observing a day of rest. To legalize about it to the point of the Sabbath's becoming a thing of torture instead of peace and joy was wrong. Legalism is wrong because it considers the act to be above the development of the person, above the consideration of the individual.

Jesus was doing a brave thing in healing the man in that place. Seated at the front of the synagogue were members of the Sanhedrin. It was their duty to see that no one who spoke in that place, and especially Jesus, would deceive the people with false doctrine. Jesus knew that they were there in order to catch him in some wrongful act or statement, but he did flinch. He called the man forward. Jesus was fully aware that his action went contrary to the interpretation of Jewish law concerning the Sabbath. He knew that such laws were exceedingly strict. Even use of medical knowledge was against the law unless it was deemed necessary to save a human life. A broken bone could not be set. A cut could not be bandaged. No ointment could be applied, for that would be part of the healing process. A strict Jew, if attacked by another, could not even defend himself on the Sabbath.

Perhaps something more needs to be said about legalism. As demanding a respect for law and order, it is good. But there must be exceptions. If a man commits murder but is judged to be insane and thus unaccountable for his deeds, this condition must be taken into consideration. Surely a child, doing something wrong out of innocence, cannot be judged the same as an adult who knowingly breaks the law. Unfortunately, the Jewish religion is built upon legalism. The law must be obeyed under any and all circumstances. Complete compliance with the law is necessary for salvation. Thus it was believed that one should not work on the Sabbath. But what is work? To some it is the means of earning one's daily bread. It can sometimes include meeting a dire emergency. If the basement is being flooded, even though it is Sunday, cannot there be a removal from the basement of those items which will be harmed by the floodwaters? It was considered wrong to go for a walk on Sunday because walking was judged to be work. But it was evident that some walking was necessary, even if it were only around the house. So what was called a Sabbath day's journey was permitted. It was about the length of a mile. Planting on the Sabbath was forbidden, so if one were tossing grain to his chickens he had to be sure that he tossed only the amount they would eat. Any grain left lying on the ground could take root and it would be considered as planted there. In our text, plucking grain to eat as one passed through a wheat field was considered in the same category as harvesting, and should not be done on the Sabbath.

Jesus said that he came not to condemn the law but to fulfill it. He was talking about a higher interpretation. Thus the law says we are not to commit adultery, but Christ pointed out that even the thought of doing so, or the lusting after a woman without committing the act, was a sin.

No one is perfect, yet the Jews said that by obeying all laws, and by that way alone, one is on the pathway to heaven. In such a case no one would get to heaven since no one is in perfect obedience; no one is perfect. But Christ came to fulfill the law. Being sinless himself, he assumed our sins and paid their penalty on the cross. Now those who link themselves to Christ by placing their faith in him have forgiveness in God's sight, and are heirs of heaven.

Sermon Material

Sunday Observance

The question of Sunday observance is before each one of us today. We do not have a law circumscribing our actions on Sunday. We are free to spend the day as we please. But what do we please? The question really is, "What good do we do on the Lord's day?" To keep the Sabbath holy is to let it produce acts of love on our part. It calls for a positive, not a negative, discipleship. People can attend church and, like the Pharisees, leave the worship of God without having love in their hearts. Hearing of God's love for us, as revealed in Jesus Christ, is to arouse love for all God's people in our own hearts.

The Sabbath Was Made For Humankind
This is not a license to do absolutely anything on the Sabbath, but only what is good for humankind. That includes rest, worship, and acts of love.

Human Need
For most people, their religion seems to be purely selfish. They are interested in their own activities, and their own salvation, but never do anything to bring others to Christ. Their idea of being religious is to be sure that they are doing the right thing: worshiping, reading the Bible, and leading a pure life. They do not comprehend the degree to which the Christian faith emphasizes concern and love for others. But, in fact, the degree to which we care about others is a measurement of the vitality of our faith.

Jesus stressed the fact that Christians should go about doing good and answer the needs of others. He warned that on the judgment day what we have done for others will be one of the criteria by which we shall be judged. He declared that when we feed the hungry, visit those who are sick or in prison, give clothing to those who need it, we are showing our love to him, because he resides in human hearts. What a challenge this is for us. We are actually commanded to be considerate of the needs of others, and to give gladly of our means and of our time. This is the Christian spirit that is responsible for the development of hospitals, homes for the poor, places to care for children without parents, and a host of other charitable organizations. A high priority in the life of a Christian is the claim of human need.

The Hand Of Christ
The scriptures often relate how Jesus used his hands to heal. He placed his hands on people who were sick and they were healed. He touched the dead and they came back to life. He touched the eyes of the blind and restored their sight, touched the ear and restored hearing, touched the tongue and caused the dumb to speak.

Some Good Things To Do On Sunday
Children sometimes complain about not having anything to do. A misinterpretation of Sunday restrictions may even lead adults

to think there is nothing left to do. But by giving it a little thought, it is surprising how many things are actually encouraged as a part of Sunday observance. Such a list follows:

1. Go to worship in the house of the Lord
2. Do good to people:
    • pick them up for church
    • give them money to purchase a good meal
    • call on the sick or lonely
    • write a letter expressing your gratitude for help or influence
3. Teach a Sunday school class
4. Sing in the choir
5. Read your Bible; this is a day when you are sure to have the time
6. Take a walk
7. Reflect on the many blessings that come from God
8. Visit with friends
9. Read a good book

Returning Evil For Good

We should do the opposite. But the Pharisees did not. They did not rejoice that a crippled man was healed. They failed to see God's power being applied by Christ, whose relationship to God was thus made clear. They were so blinded by prejudice that instead of giving thanks and rejoicing they went out of the synagogue to plan how to destroy him.

Two Views Of Religion

In this clash between Jesus and the Sanhedrin we see two contrasting views of religion. There are those who see it as ritual. It means attending a worship service in church and participating in the ritual. Or it can mean, according to this view, engaging in family devotions. That is good unless one substitutes such form for action. The purpose of devotions is not the act itself, but the influence it brings to a participant. The end result is supposed to be a more kind, gracious, sincere, and loving person. How many people think that doing their Christian duty consists of Bible reading, church attendance, and prayer, but overlook the influence this is supposed to have on one's character and personality? Religion is more than ritual; it results in changed lives, loving our neighbor as ourselves, and being stirred to action by the plight of the poor, the homeless, the sick, and those who have been brought low by tragedy. The scriptures declare that true religion consists of "visiting the fatherless and widows, and keeping oneself unspotted by the world." In contrast to ritualistic religion, Jesus went about doing good. He told the timeless story of the Good Samaritan. He showed pity for the blind, the maimed, the sorrowing, He stressed the importance of answering human need.

The Many Uses Of The Hand

If one stops to think of the severity of this man's handicap, we think of the many restrictions his withered hand would place upon him. The hand is a powerful, multi-useful instrument to help us through life. In human relations it is used to shake hands, lift a child, say "stop," say "come," form a fist, offer the sign for peace or victory, wave good-bye. In practical ways it is used to write, dress, wash or wipe dishes, prepare a meal, eat a meal. On a job the hand is used on a pick or shovel, to type, to carve or chisel, to paint. In daily life it is used to drive a car, compete in sports, play a musical instrument, sweep with a broom. All of these things and more would be denied us by the loss of a hand.

Illustrations

Obedience To Christ

Christ called to the man with the withered hand to come forward, and the man did. Christ asked him to stretch forth his hand, and he did. As a result of obeying Christ's commands the man was healed. We should learn from this that it pays to follow the directions of Christ.

Turn signals on cars are meant to be helpful in telling other drivers of our intention to make a turn. But until the action was made illegal they were wrongfully used to tell the car behind when it was safe to go around.

A coach was following a slow truck up a long grade and was grateful when the truck driver flashed a left turn signal, telling the coach he could pass. But the truck driver miscalculated the time it would take the car to pass and another car, appearing over the hill, hit the first car head-on. Several people had to be taken to the hospital.

We are offered much advice in life, some of it good, but some of it not reliable. We need to know how much we can trust the one who is advising us. Christ is all-knowing. To follow his leadership always is to do the right thing and enjoy good results.

Handicaps Other Than A Withered Hand

This miracle has a lesson for those who do not have a withered hand. There are many negative elements that try to hinder our daily activities. If we let them, these are some of the things that can have a harmful effect on us: selfishness, a loss through theft, a love of money and a trust in it, someone's deceitfulness in dealing with us. But these negative elements need not harm us. Remember, Jesus stands ready to overcome these obstacles to abundant life.

"Is It Lawful To Do Good On The Sabbath?"

Here is legalism at its worst. We are reminded of the time Jesus pointed his critics to the fact that if one of their animals fell into a pit on the Sabbath they would surely try to free the animal at once.

There were two neighbors, both widows, who had been on friendly terms. One of the women took pride in the fact that she regularly attended church and Sunday school. The other widow would have preferred to go to church but could not because of a Sunday morning job which prevented it. The first woman became critical and even complained to her pastor about her neighbor's absence from church. She did not know that her neighbor began every day, including Sunday, with private devotions of Bible reading and prayer. Nor did she fully accept the fact that her neighbor was forced to work because of financial needs. Christ said that Sunday was made for humankind and is one's to do with as one pleases. He was freeing religion from legalism. His reply would surely have been, "If you can, go to church; if you cannot, do the best you can to honor God."

Our Withered Hand

How many people might as well have a withered hand because they do not use the ones they have? They sit idly by when they should be using their hands in Christian service.

Some time ago a young woman was attacked by a knife-wielding man. She was at her door, in the darkness of night, in the courtyard of an apartment building. It was a summer night and windows were open in the various apartments. As she fought her attacker she cried out loudly for help. Many heard her anguished appeal but refused to get involved. She lay badly bleeding and in need of help when the attacker returned and resumed his vicious onslaught. She failed to endure the second attack when no one answered her plea for help. Her life could have been spared if a single person had responded to her cries for help. Answering her cries for help could have been as simple as dialing 911. But they did not do so, offering the lame excuse that they did not want to get involved. Because of their refusal to help, is not the blood of the woman who died on their hands? It is common for people to offer their sympathy to people in trouble. But Christian service demands that we take action when it is called for. Is it possible that we have withered hands and do not realize it?

"Come Here"

The man with the withered hand had to respond to Christ's invitation and approach him in order to have his hand restored. Remaining at a distance, refusing to act on the Lord's invitation, would have left him a cripple. Christ, in various ways, is continually calling us with the invitation, "Come here." To receive his inspiration and blessing we need to act on the invitation.

A pastor once said that in calling on some of his members who did not attend church, he was appalled at the variety of their excuses. He marveled at how many different excuses people gave:

1. That's my only morning to sleep.
2. I worship God in the outdoors.
3. The sermons don't give me a lift.
4. The choir sings poorly.

5. I like to get comfortable and read the Sunday morning newspaper.
6. I have to leave before church is out to get to the football game.

He reported that in his counting of different excuses he reached a total of 134. Then he stopped counting.

Far Horizons

The Pharisees criticized Christ because they were confined by their religious zeal to a narrow view of man and of love. Christ called them to view the far horizon: the encircling love of God who wishes no one to suffer and wants all to be made whole. When one is surrounded by skyscrapers in a large city he might be impressed by their height and the important business transactions that take place within them. But, at the same time, he may not realize how much they blot out his view of far-off things. Because of being surrounded by them, he cannot see the far horizon. He is unable to be thrilled by the glory of a sunrise, or of a brilliant sunset when the western sky is bathed in gold. Christ came with the desire to enlarge and widen our horizon. He wanted us to see the wide brotherhood of man, and to be interested in the welfare of others. He even gave us a view of eternity.

Miracle Six

Stilling A Storm

On that day, when evening had come, he said to them, "Let us go across to the other side." And leaving the crowd behind, they took him with them in the boat, just as he was. Other boats were with him. A great windstorm arose, and the waves beat into the boat, so that the boat was already being swamped. But he was in the stern, asleep on the cushion; and they woke him up and said to him, "Teacher, do you not care that we are perishing?" He woke up and rebuked the wind, and said to the sea, "Peace! Be still!" Then the wind ceased, and there was a dead calm. He said to them, "Why are you afraid? Have you still no faith?" And they were filled with great awe and said to one another, "Who then is this, that even the wind and the sea obey him?"

Background Material

Jesus sometimes got into a boat and headed for the farther shore in order to be free of the demands of the crowd who now followed him in great numbers. On this day he was weary from his work and from arguing with the scribes who constantly took issue with his pronouncements. He was on the Sea of Galilee, also known as Lake Gennesaret. The lake was about eight miles wide and twelve miles long, so it would take at least an hour to make the crossing. Because of his weariness Jesus lay down on a cushion in the rear of the boat and was soon sound asleep. A violent storm arose. This was typical of the Lake of Galilee. Situated as it was at the foot of mountains, the two sides of the mountains served as a funnel to carry strong winds sweeping down on the lake and violently agitating its waters. Jesus, asleep in the boat, was not aware of the storm which was causing waves to break into the boat and endanger the lives of all aboard. The disciples awoke him with words of criticism for being at rest while the company of travelers faced the possibility of death by drowning. They asked Jesus if he did not even care if they all perished. He replied with charges against their lack of faith. Then he did something which not only amazed them, but which should have restored them to full faith in Christ as the powerful Son of God. With a word or two he demanded of the elements that they stop their raging and restore a peaceful situation. The result was an amazing cessation of the storm. The disciples could express their awe at this miracle which proved the power of Christ even over the acts of nature.

We do not have to be at sea to encounter the storms and raging seas of life. A complete disruption of one's calm, replaced by upsetting uneasiness and even fear, can strike at any time, to anyone. Stress is able to upset our emotions, causing considerable damage to our sanity and health. There are spiritual storms where events transpiring in our lives sorely stress our faith. For some the bitter blow of sorrow or tragedy, striking us like a tornado, can sweep away our self-reliance. It is precisely in such situations that Christ offers to be our Savior. One has only to put one's faith in him, trusting his promise to be always near at hand with sufficient help, ready to give us courage and strength and guidance in any crisis. So Christ chided the disciples for not having more faith in him. They should have realized that with him in the boat they had nothing to fear. We need to remember that we do not walk alone through life, for Christ is with us. What reassurance that conviction can bring!

Sermon Material

Prepare For Life's Storms

Life is not always sweetness and light. We can be sure that it will bring us some bitterness along with the sweet. How foolish, then, not to be preparing oneself for the bad times that are sure to come. Are you ready for a medical diagnosis of impending death for yourself or for a loved one? Are you prepared to face loneliness in the death of a beloved spouse? What about serious financial losses, or tragedies like a house fire? Can you take adversity as well as prosperity?

Perhaps we do not give sufficient thought to the desire of Christ to minister to our deepest needs. Faith cannot be suddenly grasped in an emergency, or on the spur of the moment because our world has suddenly collapsed. It is something that is built up across a period of time. We cannot avoid many of life's troubles, but we can get ready for them by encouraging our growth in faith, by trusting in God's wisdom, in his plan for us, in his presence in every time of trouble. There are ways to achieve this, and those ways must be utilized before trouble strikes. Now is the time to encourage our growth in faith. Our faith must be nourished if it is to see us through any and all difficulties.

Jesus Cares

When we stop to think who Jesus is, it becomes amazing to us that he knows us by name and cares about what is happening to us. As a participant in the creation, Christ brought into being and rules over the far-flung universe in which we dwell. That universe stretches for billions of miles. Is it possible that he who controls the whole universe cares about so infinitesimally a part of it as we are? In the vastness of creation we are like a single grain of sand on a broad beach which stretches from New York to Florida. But God, and his son Christ, are all-knowing. Every detail of creation is permanently in his thoughts. Even a sparrow's death is within his scope of knowledge. And we are of so much more worth than a sparrow, says Christ. Let this truth sink into our consciousness. It is of great importance that we realize the extent of God's love for us. Jesus died on the cross for you. How much more must he do to exhibit the strength of his love? Yes, in all the trials of life we can experience the caring love of Christ and rejoice that we are the recipients of so great a gift of devotion.

Storms In Our Life

People who have lived through a hurricane have described what a terrible experience it is. The fact that it lasts for eight hours or more is dreadful enough. But to be cowered inside a house for that length of time is indescribably terrifying. One's mind is seized by the scary thought that the winds outside, at 190 miles per hour, might blow off the roof and the ensuing rain drench the home. The walls are sometimes blown in upon those seeking refuge from the bitter storm.

Christ is not there to still a storm, as he was on Lake Galilee. But he is always present with his believers, and he hears their prayers. To be able to call upon him in such circumstances is the only comfort and refuge some people have, and it calms the nerves as one waits out the fury of the storm.

There are many storms in human life other than those of nature. And always Christ can be called on in every time of trouble. Among a great variety of life's storms are those of anxiety, the death of a spouse or other family member, and loneliness. In compiling a list, one finds that there is no end to the numerous tragedies that can befall a human being. But always, Christ is the one sure refuge, the one we can call on in every time of trouble. He helps to overcome our difficulties by giving us strength and hope and confidence with which we are able to ride out the storm and stress.

Lake Galilee

It was a lake where a storm could rise in a hurry, and had a reputation as a dangerous lake for boating. I have been on Lake Michigan when it was very calm and fishing was a pleasure. Once, not looking westward for a time, we did not see the ominous black clouds that had suddenly appeared just above the horizon. They were racing toward us when they caught our attention. Immediately we stopped fishing and headed for shore, which was about a mile away. But well before we reached land the rain began to pour down upon us as in a cloudburst.

Galilee was famous for such winds rising rapidly and, when hitting the water, creating monstrous waves. That was because there was a deep valley running from high up in the hills down to the shore, and the wind used this area as a funnel to gather its fury. The result was often a fearful and sudden gale that created great, threatening waves.

The power to control the excesses of nature is unheard of. People simply do their best to ride out the storm. When Christ demonstrated his power over nature, it is little wonder that his followers who witnessed it were amazed beyond words. It was further proof of what an unusual person was in their midst. It furthered his claim to being more than human, to being in fact the son of God. His divinity was amply demonstrated, and when the storm abruptly ended its fury in obedience to his command, their frightened hearts became calm.

Undoubtedly A Miracle

Many people, even some preachers, have tried to explain the miracles on the basis of natural causes. The feeding of the 5,000, for instance, these detractors claim, was accomplished when people shared their "sack lunches" with those who had no food. How this could be a valid explanation tests one's credulity. How does one explain that the designated task was to feed "so many people"? Those who were present and aware of the situation called it a miracle and marveled at it.

But while such an incredulous explanation can be used to attack this miracle, one cannot find an easy explanation for the stilling of the tempest. How could a mere human force wind and waves to stop their fury abruptly at the moment of his command?

A Call For Faith

Jesus was not concerned about the threatening waves when he was awakened. But he scolded the disciples for their lack of faith. He intimates that they should have relied on the promises of God, knowing that their heavenly Father would take care of them. Do we justify our condemnation for lacking in faith when we are hit hard by some of the cruel circumstances of life?

Needing Christ To Solve Our Problems

Independence is good, but it can be carried too far. No matter how self-sufficient we may be ordinarily, there will come times when we must admit our weakness and hand over our problem to God.

This is an important step used successfully by Alcoholics Anonymous to help individuals get over their addiction to alcohol. It is now being adopted by another organization to help people get over drug addiction. There are times when we must admit that our problem is too big for us to conquer alone, and so seek help if we are to survive. Accepting God's promises is a wise step into returning to victorious living.

But at the same time, let us not limit our call upon the Eternal to times of trouble. We need to develop our spiritual growth at all times, good and bad. It is a privilege to call upon God when life is going smoothly, offering our prayers of thanksgiving. Then when trouble strikes we are ready to rely on spiritual resources.

Illustrations

"Why Are You Afraid? Have You No Faith?"

Faith and fear are enemies. You must choose one or the other, but you cannot have both.

Some boys were playing on a beach with a large beach ball. By accident the ball was thrown too high and, driven by the wind, landed in the water. No thought was given to it for a few minutes until one of the boys noticed it was going farther and farther from shore. One of the boys decided to retrieve the ball. After entering the water he realized that it was farther from shore than he had thought. Grabbing hold of the ball proved more difficult than he had expected, for it was riding high on the waves. Each time he sought to grip it, the ball slipped out of his hands. About this time he noticed that he was quite a distance from shore, and realized, too, that he was getting tired. At that point some fear gripped him as he realized that he could drown. But he was a Christian and so he spoke a brief prayer, calling on God to protect him. His prayer brought him reassurance that God would help him, and his fear was replaced by confidence. Suddenly the thought occurred to him that he should swim around the ball so that each attempt to grab it would push it in toward the shore. The plan worked. In a matter of minutes he was able to step on shore with the retrieved ball. Every Christian has the choice in every situation: succumb to fear or have faith. Learning this lesson can bring peace of mind in the many turmoils we pass through in this life.

Master Of The Storms

An elderly pastor was crossing the ocean some years ago on an ocean liner. One morning he awoke to hear the ship's foghorn blasting an ominous warning every fifteen seconds. Going out on deck he saw that the fog was so thick that he could see only a few feet in front of him. The fearful thought crossed his mind that under these circumstances there could be a fatal crash of two ships and all aboard would drown in the mighty ocean far from land. He made his way forward on the deck until he could see the ship's bridge. It was very reassuring to see that standing on the bridge was the ship's captain, a man of many ocean crossings. The figure of the ship's captain standing at his post gave great reassurance to the minister as the vessel crawled ahead in the fog.

How reassuring it is to the Christian to know that amid the storms of life Christ is alert to our difficulties. He who took command of the mighty waves on the Sea of Galilee will answer our cry as we call upon him when the waves of life roll over us.

"Have You No Faith?"

People go through life with contrasting attitudes. For some, life can be faced courageously. Others seem to cower constantly before ills that are either real or imagined. Some interesting statistics along this line were issued by the famous Mayo Clinic. They issued a report that anxiety is one of humanity's greatest foes. Their report stated that one person in every ten will have a nervous breakdown sometime in his life, induced by worry. Even more startling was their statement that one person in twenty will spend some time in a mental institution. They declared that more than half of the hospital beds in America are occupied by people whose basic trouble is due to nervousness, induced by anxiety. It was reported further that of 15,000 people treated at their clinic for stomach disorders, no physical basis for their trouble existed; fear and worry had caused their illness.

The Cross Destroys Worry (Anxiety)

A wedding rehearsal was being conducted at a large church. Among the participants was a six-year-old flower girl. She had difficulty coming down the lengthy center aisle. She was tense, took little steps, and kept her head down. Her mother knew that criticism would only make her more tense and awkward. There was a large cross on the church's altar so the mother suggested that her daughter march down the aisle looking up at that cross and thinking about how much Jesus loved her. The idea worked very well and at the wedding the little flower girl made a deep impression on the congregation. There is a lesson here for all adults as well. Keeping our thoughts on the cross will cause our troubles to diminish, lighten our burdens, and restore a glow to life.

"And They Woke Him"

There were six cities in ancient Israel which were designated as cities of refuge. When someone took a human life without premeditation or malice he could flee to one of these cities and there be safe from retribution. Tradition tells that once each year the roads leading to such a city were cleared of rocks and debris to make it easier for a man who was fleeing for his life to reach the haven of safety. Christ is God's great haven of safety, a refuge from life's turmoils, sin, and death.

"Do You Not Care If We Perish?"

God indeed cares, and sent his Son to keep us from perishing because of our sins. The story is told of an ancient king who dearly loved his son but wanted him to grow in character by facing up to life's hardships. So he sent him out into life to meet whatever troubles might come his way. The young man thought he was alone and grew with each difficulty he met. He did not know that his father's love had caused the king to send out a group of strong and brave knights to look after his son. Through the dark nights when he could hear the howling of wild beasts, the prince had no idea that the knights were near at hand for his protection. In life we may think we are alone. We need to remember that a loving and caring heavenly Father is keeping watch over his own. We are never alone. God cares and he is watching over us.

* * *

When trouble arises, where, or to whom, do we turn? If sickness strikes, we turn to a doctor, or perhaps a pharmacist, who will give us the right medicine. When a marriage turns sour, couples are advised to see a marriage counselor. The disciples had a better plan. Caught in a wild storm on the sea which threatened their lives, they turned to Christ. Should we not use this source of help more often? For instance, many physical ills are caused by anxiety and worry, usually about something that will not even occur. Christ could well be the answer to such ills. He promises to ease our burdens. Putting anxiety into Christ's hands and trusting in him could eradicate many of them. And often it is the lack of any spiritual influence in the home that disrupts harmony and causes marital problems in the home and the breakup of the family. Young people who go wrong could have avoided many lures and pitfalls if they had been introduced to Christ. The Psalmist wisely pointed to the need to turn to God, especially in times of trouble. He emphasized God's interest in each one of us when he wrote his message from God: "Call on me in the day of trouble; I will deliver you, and you shall glorify me" (Psalm 50:15).

"A Great Storm Arose"

Storms at sea have been a part of human experience from the beginning of time. On Christopher Columbus' journey home after discovering the New World, a storm threatened to sink his ship. He was less concerned for his life than he was fearful that his tremendous discovery would remain unknown. So he hurriedly put the message in several bottles which were cast into the sea in the hope that someday they might be picked up on a shore. He did not want his splendid achievement to be lost. There are many storms in life

75

other than those at sea. When they occur, we need to commit our life to Christ, who can pilot us over life's "tempestuous seas."

Call Upon The Lord

Daniel Defoe in the well-known book *Robinson Crusoe* bases his story on the need to call upon God in time of trouble. Crusoe had long been isolated on a small island following a shipwreck. He had come to believe firmly that he was the only human being on the island. But one day as he went to the beach to get his boat he was startled to see the footprint of a man in the sand. Crusoe concluded that it was the footprint of a savage. In great fear he hurried back to his cabin. There, while lying on his bed, trembling with fear as he thought of savages, he suddenly thought of the words of scripture: "Call on me in the day of trouble and I will deliver you, and you will glorify me." This thought was of such comfort that Crusoe rose cheerfully from his bed. He exulted in the great comfort that the opportunity to pray to God for deliverance gave him. He returned to his normal daily life without fear.

Conquering Our Own Storms

Modern submarines cannot easily be caught without warning of an impending disaster. They have the use of radar, and by means of radio can keep in touch with their headquarters and hear the weather reports. We, too, can tune in to forecasts about the weather and be warned of severe thunderstorms or winter storms of snow and ice. But there are some storms of a different nature, whose advance warnings we must heed. When we wonder if our child is becoming a secret addict to drugs or alcohol, we are told that there are certain signs to look for. These include lowering grades in school, or even skipping school, irritability, aggressiveness to an extreme, threats to run away from home, or to commit suicide. Perhaps when this happens, anxious parents wonder where to turn. This is a time when Christ can come to our rescue in the storms of life. We need to expose our minds and souls to him who promises to bring us life abundant. The closer we stay to him, the greater is the help he can offer us.

Life's Storms

Victor Hugo, in his story "Ninety-Three," tells of a ship caught in a dangerous storm on the high seas. At the height of the storm, the frightened sailors heard a terrible crashing noise below the deck. They knew at once that this new noise came from a cannon, part of the ship's cargo, that had broken loose. It was moving back and forth with the swaying of the ship, crashing into the side of the ship with terrible impact. Knowing that it could cause the ship to sink, two brave sailors volunteered to make the dangerous attempt to retie the loose cannon. They knew the danger of a shipwreck from the cannon was greater than the fury of the storm.

That is like human life. Storms of life may blow about us, but it is not these exterior storms that pose the gravest danger. It is the terrible corruption that can exist within us which can overwhelm us. Our only hope lies in conquering that wild enemy. Unfortunately sin is something we cannot cure by ourselves. It takes the power of God's love, as revealed in Jesus Christ. He is our only hope of stilling the tempest that can harm our souls and cripple our lives.

Miracles Seven And Eight

Healing An Issue Of Blood
Healing The Ruler's Daughter

When Jesus had crossed again in the boat to the other side, a great crowd gathered around him; and he was by the sea. Then one of the leaders of the synagogue named Jairus came and, when he saw him, fell at his feet and begged him repeatedly, "My little daughter is at the point of death. Come and lay your hands on her, so that she may be made well, and live." So he went with him.

And a large crowd followed him and pressed in on him. Now there was a woman who had been suffering from hemorrhages for twelve years. She had endured much under many physicians, and had spent all that she had; and she was no better, but rather grew worse. She had heard about Jesus, and came up behind him in the crowd and touched his cloak, for she said, "If I but touch his clothes, I will be made well." Immediately her hemorrhage stopped; and she felt in her body that she was healed of her disease. Immediately aware that power had gone forth from him, Jesus turned about in the crowd and said, "Who touched my clothes?" And his disciples said to him, "You see the crowd pressing in on you; how can you say, 'Who touched me?'" He looked all around to see who had done it. But the woman, knowing what had happened to her, came in fear and trembling, fell down before him, and told him the whole truth. He said to her, "Daughter, your faith has made you well; go in peace, and be healed of your disease."

While he was still speaking, some people came from the leader's house to say, "Your daughter is dead. Why trouble the teacher any further?" But overhearing what they said, Jesus said to the leader of the synagogue, "Do not fear, only believe." He allowed no one to follow him except Peter, James, and John, the brother of James. When they came to the house of the leader of the synagogue, he saw a commotion, people weeping and wailing loudly. When he had entered, he said to them, "Why do you make a commotion and weep? The child is not dead but sleeping."

And they laughed at him. Then he put them all outside, and took the child's father and mother and those who were with him, and went in where the child was. He took her by the hand and said to her, "Talitha cum," which means, "Little girl, get up!" And immediately the girl got up and began to walk about (she was twelve years of age). At this they were overcome with amazement. He strictly ordered that no one should know this, and told them to give her something to eat.

Background Material

Jesus' performance of miracles was now assuming a rapid pace. Great crowds now came to meet him wherever he went, and they brought with them their sick and lame to have the Master apply his healing powers. Here Jesus sets out, in response to a plea from one of the rulers of the synagogue, who asks him to come to his home to heal a sick daughter; on the way, still another miracle comes to pass. The interruption was unusual. A miracle was performed without a request. A woman who had suffered for years had some kind of bleeding problem. Without asking anything of Christ, she simply got up behind him in the crowd and touched his garment. She had suffered long and found no cure, and had spent all her money on a string of physicians. But she believed her long quest for healing would come to an end if she simply touched Christ's garment. And by doing so, she was healed. Apparently she was one of the thousands of people who had heard of Jesus and his miraculous cures. Legend has it that she traveled a considerable distance to receive a cure. This would show how great a distance the fame of Christ had spread. But she had reached the point of feeling there was no hope for her, having been to many doctors without a beneficial result. Upon hearing of Christ, she regained her hope and had confidence that he could heal her. So she made the journey to where he was.

Perhaps she was bashful, or had such a profound appreciation of Christ's divinity, but something kept her from having the courage to face Christ. But so strong was her confidence in him that she reasoned that it would be enough simply to touch Christ's robe. So when she joined the throng surrounding him, she worked her way up through the crowd to a spot directly behind the Master. Then in great faith she reached out and touched his garment. Instantly a power flowed from him into her body, and she was at last cured of her ailment.

Jesus felt the healing power flow from him and turned around. Why he would ask who touched him is a matter of conjecture. Perhaps he wanted to direct the attention of many to what had just happened. But his question baffled the disciples, for they thought it was not at all unlikely that many had pressed up against him in the crowd. His question made the healed woman realize that Christ knew what had happened, so she came forth, with fear and trembling, not knowing whether or not she was to be rebuked for her action. But Jesus did not scold; instead he pronounced a blessing, telling the woman that her faith had made her whole.

This whole episode was an interlude in Christ's response to Jairus' request to come to his house and heal his sick daughter. If the delay in doing so, caused by the healing of the woman with the issue of blood, had previously been considered trivial, it now took on enormous proportions. For the news came from Jairus' home, spoken in blunt language, "Your daughter is dead." This must have caused some to be critical of Christ, saying in their hearts, "You have delayed too long." They even said, "Don't trouble the teacher any further." What a blow that news was. But it did not perturb Jesus. He simply ignored their acceptance of death and told Jairus not to worry, but to continue to have faith.

Jesus sensed that many in the crowd around him were there merely from curiosity, and he had no desire to have the miracles detract from his message about the kingdom of God. So he wanted to get away from the gawkers and be alone with his disciples. So taking with him only Peter, James, and John, he accompanied Jairus to his home. What he saw at the home, however, was appalling. News of the death had spread, and friends and neighbors in great numbers had come together to join in the sorrowing. Jesus approached them and as much as asked them, "What is all this noise and commotion about? There is no death here. The young lady is not dead, only sleeping." This led to open contempt toward the Lord, and they scoffed at him and showed him their scorn. How often "little" people satisfy their egos by scoffing at those who are greater than they. It costs them nothing to do so, and takes little effort. Still one is appalled to think that some people were so crude and rude as to scoff at the Son of God. But this did not deter Jesus from carrying out his intentions. He emptied the house of the crowd, except for the immediate family. Then he took the hand of the dead girl and spoke to her, asking her to get up. When she returned quickly to life and obeyed the command of Christ, those who were present were absolutely stunned. We are all so helpless in the face of death. Yet here was one who obviously held complete power and authority over this enemy of all humankind. They were asked, however, not to go around telling people of this miracle. This was in line with what had been stated previously: Christ did not want to attract a large number of gawkers who were not interested in his spiritual message.

Sermon Material

Jesus Helps Where Others Fail

The woman with the issue of blood had been suffering for twelve years. Throughout that time she had gone to many doctors, one after another, but not one of them could heal her. We all know of people today who go from doctor to doctor, seeking a cure for their ailment, but receiving little, if any, help. No doubt each doctor she had visited prescribed one of the odd treatments which were recommended in those days. Perhaps they recommended stringents and salves, which proved futile. Some could even have been outlandish, playing upon superstition. For instance, the Talmud, we are told, offers the advice of carrying in a cloth the ashes of an ostrich egg. Giving her attempts at a cure one more try, she traveled to where Christ was, for she had heard of his unusual healing powers.

While she had faith in Christ's abilities, she was also aware of his greatness and reputation. Perhaps she was bashful or lacking in self-regard. At any rate, she did not approach Christ directly but decided it would be enough simply to touch his garment. Joining the crowd following Christ, she worked her way up to a position directly behind him. When the opportunity arose she reached out her hand and touched the Lord, and instantly her long-time search for a cure was answered. She was made whole.

As we make our way through life on earth there are many things which weigh us down. We are troubled about our finances. We have health concerns. We meet up with disappointments and defeats. There are discouragements along the way. One has to wonder how some people think they can overcome all these negatives alone. Christ, who can be of immense help, offers to come to us with his aid. "Come unto me," he pleads, as he is often passed by. But he stands ready to hear our prayers, our calls for help. He is eager to lift our burdens, to forgive our sins, to give us his companionship as we meet the troubles of life. It is good if we finally go to Christ in the end. But why should we delay and make him the final hope? Why should we not practice the presence of Christ and receive his blessings throughout our lifetime?

The Need For Faith

The woman with the issue of blood had faith in Christ. She is described as saying, "If I touch even his garments, I shall be made well." And Christ's response emphasizes the importance of faith, for he says, "Daughter, your faith has made you well." Many times in performing a miracle, Christ stressed the element of faith. When Christ was followed by two blind men seeking a cure, he asked them, "Do you believe that I am able to do this?" And in healing them he declared, "According to your faith, be it done unto you."

Christ's Many Miracles

By counting the miracles performed by Christ as recounted in the four Gospels, one reaches the count of 35. This is a very large number, but it is far from the grand total. Many more were reported elsewhere. And as one Gospel writer declares: "If all the marvelous works of Christ were told, the world could not hold all the books." His lifetime on earth was short, but he went around doing good, and the sum total of his great deeds is overwhelming.

Prejudice

The man who came to Jesus on behalf of his daughter was a deeply committed Jew. He was a leader of the local synagogue, chosen because of his unquestioned Jewish faith and loyalty. On the other hand, Christ was one whom devout Jews hated because he represented, so they thought, a threat to their religious practices and devotion. He was held to be one whom an orthodox Jew should avoid because he was a rank outsider, even a heretic. But if the ruler of the synagogue held any prejudice toward Christ, he suppressed it and sought the help of Christ.

How often prejudice cuts us off from the full utilization and enjoyment of life. It is so restrictive. In contrast to the confining power of prejudice, a good life offers much variety. It can be like a flower garden in which flowers of different colors grow side by side, each adding to the total beauty. Christ brushed aside all prejudice based on race by saying that all humans are of one blood.

Prejudice can cut us off from many privileges in life. It can deny us rich friendships with those of another color or social status. If the president of the synagogue had let prejudice for another religion rule him, he would not have come to Christ and his daughter would not have been healed and restored to life.

Prejudice is a judgment reached before the facts are known. It is a verdict reached even before the evidence is considered. It is blind!

"They Laughed At Him"

This incident shows how easily our scorn can be misdirected. To think that people would laugh at Christ. How mistaken they were. We should avoid being scornful, as it is usually based on ignorance. The scoffers did not realize that the man at whom they were laughing was the Christ, the Son of God, the long-awaited Messiah. We can so easily reveal our own ignorance when we adopt a scornful attitude.

Because of their scorn and lack of faith, Jesus was not able to perform many miracles in his hometown of Nazareth. Elsewhere he could restore sight to the blind, heal the sick, raise the dead, and be widely acclaimed. But here in the house of the ruler of the synagogue the people laughed and rejected him. When this type of action takes place, who is the loser? Surely those who take "offense at him" and reject him with laughter and scorn.

Their lack of confidence in the supernatural powers of Christ sprang from their familiarity about Christ and his parents. They knew his carpenter father and had seen Jesus growing up. There is a lesson here. We must not let our familiarity lead us to overlook the talented youth in our midst. Jesus declared, "A prophet is not without honor, save in his own country." The young people around us will be assuming positions of responsibility in tomorrow's world. They are the future doctors, lawyers, teachers, writers, and political successes. To gain for them the necessary self-confidence, we must contemplate their future accomplishments and show them our respect. It is essential to avoid making judgments based on external qualities rather than on native worth.

It is also true that we must not get laughed out of our religious convictions, but remain loyal to Christ in spite of any scoffers who would try to ridicule us.

Life After Death

Death is humanity's greatest foe. It is a serious threat because it is unavoidable. Sooner or later everyone now living will have to undergo the termination of earthly life. Because of this, an answer to death is eagerly sought. Does it really end all, or is our existence a continuing one beyond the grave?

Christ brought many blessings through his teachings and life on earth, but the greatest gift which he offers is that of eternal life. He creates and strengthens our belief in eternity. During his ministry he claimed to have power over death, and on three occasions he proved it. This miracle, performed on the daughter of Jairus, is one of them. It verifies the statement of Christ, "I am the resurrection and the life. He that believeth in me, though he were dead, shall yet live." His own resurrection was the crowning proof of his authority over death. Christ died on a cross, before many witnesses. To make sure of his demise, the Roman soldier thrust a spear into his side. He was buried in a tomb. But three days later he came back to life on earth, to be seen by scores of people. To the disciple who doubted his return, he gave undeniable proof that it was so. Christianity has so much to offer, but its most highly prized gift is the assurance of eternal life. The miracle of raising the daughter of Jairus from the dead substantiates our confidence in Christ, the Lord of Life.

Pride

Everyone has heard the axiom, "Pride goes before a fall." One of the demands of Christianity is the willingness to pray, "God have mercy on me, a sinner." The Bible warns us against thinking more highly of ourselves than we ought to think. It pictures us honestly as sinners in need of a savior.

The ruler of the synagogue would have been a man deeply satisfied with, if not actually proud of, his distinguished position of distinction. Great power and influence came with his title. Therefore, it was certainly demanding for him to seek a favor from Christ. Yet because he refused to be ruled by pride, he found the help his sick daughter so desperately needed. This is a lesson for all of us. We need to accept the spirit of the hymn which describes us in the phrase, "that saves a wretch like me."

What We Miss Through Indifference To Christ

Those who scoffed at Christ were asked to leave and could not be present when the miracle was performed. They could see the result, and they did not witness the remarkable act. We, too, lose great advantages by indifference to or rejection of Christ. A few:

1. the companionship of the Divine
2. the conviction and assurance of eternal life
3. the guidance and inspiration of Christ's life and teachings
4. the comfort which Christ can bring in time of sorrow
5. the inspiration to live at the highest level
6. the joy of knowing that we are loved
7. the many resources of prayer
8. the blessedness of hope, produced by faith

And how many more advantages?

Illustrations

Death

Have you ever been in a situation where you thought you would die? Several years ago a veteran missionary was in a plane that was circling over Detroit and unable to land because of fog. As the plane's fuel ran low and the danger of a crash landing became more apparent, the missionary got out paper and pencil and jotted down his last will and testament. He wrote: "There is peace, perfect peace in my heart and soul. Life with Christ is the way to live. Now in this hour there is assurance that God is underneath all the uncertainties of human experience. So I rest in God."

We must all face the possibility of death. It is certain. Have we found the way to face this prospect peacefully?

Seek A Total Life

Some people die completely. Their lives are over. They are buried. But others who appear to be alive are only partly so. While they still have physical life, they are dead to so much that is vital in this world.

My wife and I were strolling through the halls of a great museum in Europe. Someone had let two stray dogs into the building and they were roaming around. We conjectured how they lacked entirely the ability to appreciate the marvelous works of art hanging on the walls. Not only are dogs "dead" to the world of fine paintings, but they are dead to great music, to the world of science, of religion, even of human realities. We human beings can be "dead" to so much, or we can take advantage of our endless opportunities to explore new worlds. Like the young girl restored to life by Christ, we can be awakened, by him, to so much that is truly wonderful in life. Christ came to bring us abundant living. That means life to the full, life with a capital L.

Your God Is Too Small

The woman with the issue of blood was filled with faith. She really believed that by simply touching the hem of Christ's garment a miracle could be effected. She is an example to us of great faith, and how it is rewarded.

We may be committed and praying Christians, but do we think large enough thoughts about God? Do we really believe that God can do anything? A book has been written with the startling title, *Your God Is Too Small.* That title is a wake-up challenge to all of us. If we believe in an all-powerful God, it should be reflected in the confidence with which we turn to God in prayer. "Ask and you shall receive," Jesus urged. Yet we often wonder whether or not God can really help us. Wake up to the power which God possesses, power he has promised to use on our behalf.

A Father's Love

Jairus represents a father's love for his children. He was a devout Jew, the leader of his synagogue, and Jesus was considered a religious outcast. But Jairus did not hesitate to seek out Christ and implore his help for his dying daughter. He would do anything to save her life.

Recently the newspapers carried an account of a fire that destroyed a home. The father woke up to a smoke-filled house and hurried his family to safety. But while standing in his front yard he realized that one child was missing and apparently was still in the burning home. It was very dangerous to reenter the flaming building and firemen tried to dissuade him from going back into the home. But he went anyway and was badly burned, he did rescue his son. When asked about his actions, the father said he would rather die than live and know that he had not attempted to save his little son.

God is our Father and his love for us is very great. He was willing to make the great sacrifice of his only begotten Son in order to save the world, to save you and me. How thankful we should be that we have a heavenly Father who knows us, loves us, and watches over us. Even death cannot separate us from his love. Christ, with his heavenly power, brought back to life the daughter of Jairus. God will bring us safely through the valley of the shadow of death, into the kingdom of everlasting life.

The Healing Power Of Faith

The woman with the issue of blood had faith that by contact with Christ she could be cured. All around us in daily life are examples of people who, by faith, are overcoming life's difficulties.

A telephone linesman was up a pole when the pole, which was held in place only by wire stays, fell over him and he was dashed to the ground. His insides were badly crushed and as he was rushed to the hospital there was little hope that he could survive. A pastor learned of the accident when the man's wife called from the hospital. She said that the very best surgeons in the community had operated but found that he was beyond repair and they had given up all hope. She had been informed that her husband would die within the hour. She asked the pastor to hurry to the hospital to baptize her husband before he died. The pastor entered the sickroom to find a patient with the color of death, too weak to speak. Quickly the pastor explained that God loved the patient. In a few words he explained that baptism makes one a child of God whose sins are forgiven through Christ's death on the cross. Then he asked the patient if he wished to be baptized. The man was too weak to do more than slightly shake his head in consent. After the baptism the pastor asked the wife again if two of the best doctors in the community had declared that the man would die within the hour. The answer was yes. As the pastor left he asked the wife to call him when death came. The pastor got no call that day, nor through the following night. So the next morning he called the wife, who told him that her husband was still alive and some of his color had returned. He fell asleep after the pastor's visit, something he had not done since the accident, and he even ate some food for the first time. The man recovered completely and in a few months was once again climbing telephone poles. All medical help had proven of no avail, but evidently the introduction of faith, and the spiritual dimension, had caused the man to rally. It has been well said, that "more things are wrought by prayer than this world dreams of."

Reach Out

The woman with the issue of blood was healed because she reached out to Christ, reached to touch his garment. We, too, can reach out to Christ and as a result receive innumerable blessings. In fact, throughout our life there are so many things that we can possess if we only reach out to secure them. Many of the greatest names in history would have remained unknown if they had failed to reach out when opportunity presented itself. Examples of this include William Shakespeare, who was the son of a bankrupt butcher and a mother who could not even spell her own name. The great musician, Beethoven, was not born to international acclaim, for his father was a well-known drunkard and his mother was a sickly person, afflicted with tuberculosis. Michael Faraday was born over a stable where his father carried on the trade of a blacksmith, and his mother earned some money in the drudgery of a cleaning woman. With only a second grade education Michael Faraday became one of the most productive and famous scientists of all time. His discoveries in the field of electricity are considered the basis for all progress in that important area of human knowledge.

We have so much within reach if we only seek it. This is especially true when one reaches out to accept the offer of abundant living which Christ offers to everyone.

Miracle Nine

Healing A Deaf-Mute

Then he returned from the region of Tyre, and went by way of Sidon towards the Sea of Galilee, in the region of the Decapolis. They brought to him a deaf man who had an impediment in his speech; and they begged him to lay his hand on him. He took him aside in private, away from the crowd, and put his fingers into his ears, and he spat and touched his tongue. Then looking up to heaven, he sighed and said to him, "Ephphatha," that is, "Be opened." And immediately his ears were opened, his tongue was released, and he spoke plainly. Then Jesus ordered them to tell no one; but the more he ordered them, the more zealously they proclaimed it. They were astounded beyond measure, saying, "He has done everything well; he even makes the deaf to hear and the mute to speak."

Background Material

It is rather strange that Mark is the only Evangelist to record this particular miracle of Jesus. It is believed that the other Gospel writers had Mark's writings in hand when they wrote their Gospels. And this was a double miracle, a healing of both deafness and of a speech impediment. All the more wonder that Mark is the only one to relate this action.

Another area of conjecture concerns the man's speech impediment. Although he is often called a deaf-mute, the scriptures refer to his trouble as an impediment. Apparently he could talk but could not be easily understood. This could have been a result of his deafness, as those who cannot hear their own voice are not able to make some necessary vocal adjustments in order to be clearly understood.

The account of this miracle begins with some details of the course of Christ's travels. And this has led to some criticism of Mark's text by those who are willing to argue with scripture. To go from Tyre to Sidon through the region of Decapolis makes one turn to a map of the area. Then one learns that Jesus intended ultimately to make his way south but instead appears to have headed north. There are logical reasons for this deviation. Have not we, ourselves, sometimes turned aside from our intended course to answer an urge to visit another spot? Is it not possible that Jesus was unwilling to postpone any longer visiting those places in the north, before going south again? It can be noted that the Decapolis, a name meaning ten towns, was a group of villages that had banded together, perhaps for mutual defense.

Certainly the much-extended journey gave Christ more time to be with his disciples before returning to the press of large crowds. This trip is said to have taken eight months, thus making it worthy of mention in Mark's writing. During this time Christ could have given his disciples considerable teaching, as well as increasing their devotion to his cause. It could well have been intended as a time for their development of insight into Christ's character and for their growing commitment to their Lord.

A group of his friends (we do not know how many) brought a man to Christ for his healing. The man had lost his hearing and, in addition, could not be understood when he tried to speak. The friends had faith in Christ's power to heal. They asked the Lord to lay his hands on their friend. For centuries it had been believed that the hands could somehow be a means of passing power from one person to another. On more than one occasion Christ healed by the use of his hands. Even today, in the ordination service of young pastors, already-ordained pastors participating in the ceremony place their hands upon the one being ordained. The thought behind this action is that in this manner the power and authority of one generation is passed on to the next. In other circumstances, the massage relies on the use of hands as a therapeutic action.

In response to the plea for help, Jesus went aside with the man who had been stone-deaf. As has been pointed out previously, leaving the crowd behind would separate Christ from those who came out of idle curiosity just to see a miracle performed. It has also been suggested that Christ stepped out of the sight and hearing of the crowd because his time for public acclaim had not yet arrived. At any rate, he performed the miracle in private.

Apparently the man was well-known, and his infirmity had been witnessed by many. Though they did not see the miracle performed, when Christ first put his finger into the man's ear and said, "Ephphatha," and then loosened the man's tongue, they knew at once that the miracle had been performed. But since Christ did not yet desire or seek public acclaim, he charged the crowd not to tell anyone about what had transpired. But people like to talk and to bear news. So Christ's admonition was ignored and they told about it everywhere.

Sermon Material

The Shortcomings Of Deafness

We who can hear are guilty of not comprehending the difficulty faced by one who is deaf. We hear many things without stopping to think how fortunate we are and how unfortunate it is to lose one's hearing. The deaf cannot hear the birds singing their words of cheer. They cannot talk to others and hear their reply. The world of children's voices is foreign to them, as well as the voices of all their loved ones. Music can be a wonderful source of inspiration, but when one is deaf this is another area where one is completely shortchanged.

All these shortcomings are burdens to be borne today, but this man was deaf in a time when the restrictions of such an impediment were multiplied. This miracle was performed in a day when there were no other means of communication, such as sign language. There were no pads of paper on which to write messages, and most people of that time were not sufficiently educated to be able to write anyway. Such modern inventions as e-mail were undreamed of. In many ways a deaf man in that day was pitifully handicapped in trying to communicate with others.

The Improper Use Of Hearing

Those of us who hear have the power to listen and to heed what we want. Some folks use this freedom for good, others do not. For instance, there is such a thing as spiritual deafness, brought on by a willful refusal to hear certain voices. God is speaking to us through the scriptures. Do we listen? Our conscience is constantly urging us to do what is right, but do we always accept its prodding? Why do people listen to others, but not to God? When Jesus spoke some of his matchless truths he would conclude by saying, "Blessed are they that hear." He knew that in some cases his words were falling on "deaf" ears. If we are in need of healing of spiritual deafness, Christ is waiting to heal us, just as he did long ago in the performance of his miracles.

Using Spittle To Cure

Spitting is somewhat distasteful in modern society. People find a person who spits in public to be revolting. But in Christ's time a special, healing power was attached to human spittle. So-called health cures come and go. This one has disappeared. But different cures are "peddled" for a time and then discarded. This was not the only time when Christ would spit, then take the saliva and use it in the healing process. Perhaps this was done to strengthen the faith of the one being healed, since he would know of the widespread belief in the healing power of spittle.

"They Brought ... A Man"

We are told that as the population of the United States increases, church membership remains the same. Therefore, the percentage of Christians in our nation is slowly dropping. Various methods are used by pastors and congregations to stem the tide of falling membership and to produce membership growth. But most of the methods so employed are short-lived and result in failure.

A study of new members who join churches has revealed that the vast majority of them were moved to join a church because someone invited them. This is by far the best method of achieving results. The personal invitation is the most effective tool of evangelism. Whom have you invited to your church? Are we letting

Christ down, and are we unmoved by the decline in church membership? What do we think of the steady rise and growth of cults and oriental religions?

The deaf-mute was healed because he was brought to Christ. We do not know why he did not come of his own accord. There are people around us today who, when asked why they do not attend any church, will answer, "Because we have never been asked." Who is there to whom you should be giving a friendly invitation to attend your church? Who is there in your wide social circle who can honestly say that they have never been asked to a service of worship, to meet Christ, the Creator and Savior of the world?

Stepping Aside With Christ

According to the account, Jesus took the man aside to heal him. We, too, can step aside from the daily routine to spend time with Christ. Such opportunities lie in worship, in daily devotions, in Bible reading, and in prayer, to mention a few. And the benefits that result will always be apparent. In the present age, especially with so many blatant calls for our attention coming from television, the news media, and magazines, it is more important than ever to set aside time for Christ in our lives.

Looking Up To God

Jesus looked up before performing this miracle of healing. We may tend to forget that the power which Christ possessed was not of himself, but came from God. Christ kept vigorously alive this contact with his source of power by continually looking to God and seeking his gifts. It was this relationship with his heavenly Father that produced a flow of power through Christ, enabling him to work his miracles. So closely and so constantly did Christ maintain this contact that he could say, "The Father and I are one."

It is a great attribute, and indeed a human one, to proclaim one's self-sufficiency. But there are limits to this bravado. The most successful people on earth, people who are loaded with talent and apparently able to accomplish so much on their own, have hidden and severe limits which sometimes bring them down to defeat. As believers we can go outside ourselves to receive the inspiration, energy, will, and guidance that together create success. We are born to be dependent on God and to give him the credit for whatever success we achieve. Looking up to God should be a characteristic of every Christian, for we know that of ourselves we can do little, but with God's help we can do all things.

Ephphatha — Be Opened

The word *ephphatha*, which Christ used in opening the man's ears to full hearing, is an Aramaic word meaning "to open." Christ called himself a door which we are to open, and in so doing receive many blessings. This metaphor opens up an opportunity to consider many such blessings:

1. Christ closes the door of loneliness and opens the door to his rich fellowship.
2. Christ closes the door of fear, and opens the door of faith.
3. Christ closes the door to bitterness, hate, and grudges, and opens the door to love.
4. Christ closes the door to despair and opens the door to hope.
5. Christ closes the door to helplessness and opens the door to God's blessings.
6. Christ closes the door to materialistic grasping and opens the door of the spiritual world.
7. Christ closes the door to death and opens the door to eternal life.
8. Christ closes the door to ignorance and opens the door to truth.

Do Not Tell

Several times in the performance of his miracles recorded in this book, Christ admonished the one who was healed to be quiet about it. The main reason for this command, it has been pointed out, was that Jesus was promoting a spiritual message and did not want this purpose clouded over by those who would come to him simply to witness a miracle. In this case there was an added reason for requesting that his good deed not be noised about. It was in this very geographic area that a short time earlier the crowds had been so impressed by Christ that they had tried by force to make him king. He had rejected such overtures then and did not want the scene to be repeated.

He Has Done All Things Well
"Well done" is the highest praise that a United States sailor can receive from one of his superiors. In this instance, high praise is being heaped on Christ by those who proclaimed, "He has done all things well." This was after they had heard his message, witnessed his life, and watched him perform miracles. We all like to receive praise. As Christians it must be our aim to let others see in our daily lives an example of faith, love, and service in Christ's name. Whether or not we receive earthly praise, we can look forward to receiving praise from above. Our ultimate goal should be to avoid condemnation on the day of judgment. Instead we count on our faith in Christ, and a life lived in obedience to him, to win for us the ultimate reward, the crown of life.

Illustrations

"And His Ears Were Opened"
There are so many things in life today that require the use of our hearing. We listen to the telephone, to the radio and television, to signals and warning sounds. A great blessing for the hearing-impaired today is the hearing aid. None of the above were available to the man whom Jesus healed of deafness. There is a big difference, however, between listening and hearing. Many people are good hearers who fail, however, really to listen to what they hear. They turn down good advice or fail to follow through on what they hear. We hope that the man who could now hear listened to the message of Christ and became a Christian. He and we have the same need — to be healed of spiritual deafness. God is constantly speaking to us. We can hear his voice, but do we listen? He is calling us to live a good life. He asks us to trust in him. He speaks to us through our conscience about human needs, about suffering humanity, about racial injustice, about starving multitudes. He calls us to do our part in relieving the suffering of the poor and

needy. He calls us to come out of our self-centeredness and in our small way to be our brother's keeper. If we listen to Christ's voice, we will hear those calls for help. It is help we can give if we both hear and listen. Have we received the miracle predicted by Isaiah, "The ears of the deaf shall be unstopped"? (Isaiah 35:5).

"And He Charged Them Strictly That No One Should Know This"

Christ had his reasons for keeping news of this miracle from spreading. He did not want to attract a crowd of the curious, eager to witness a miracle, but rather to attract those who had a spiritual hungering so that he could build his kingdom. And by now his fame had spread over a wide area, so he did not need a miracle to attract attention to his message. His kingdom could now expand on its own strength.

Without giving it much thought we live in an atmosphere where the air is filled with music and speech. By means of a radio or television we catch that music and those verbal messages. But we have to turn on our radio or television or else what is in the air is unknown to us.

God has given us his Word. It is preached in churches; it can be read in the Bible. But it is necessary that we put ourselves in touch. We must listen, not with our ears only, but with the heart, in order to receive that Word. Examine yourself. Are you listening to God?

Shutting Out Our Needs

The deaf-mute was completely shut out of most of life. He could not hear others talk. He could not hear beautiful music or listen to the sounds of nature like the chirping of birds or of crickets at eventide. The joyous cries of children at play meant nothing to him. Neither could he communicate with people, for he could not speak. To express thanks to others, and to God, using verbal sounds was impossible. He could not give expression to love. He was shut out from the world which is so familiar to us.

In ancient Greece it was customary for peddlers who walked the streets with their wares to cry out, "What do you lack?" Their idea was to let people know they were in the vicinity, but also to rouse the curiosity of people who would come out of their houses to see what the peddler was selling. It might be something they lacked and needed, or simply something they desired. "What do you lack?" might well be a question we should ask ourselves. We may have sight and hearing, but what do we lack? Take an honest inventory of yourself. Have you found contentment? Are you close enough to God to receive his guidance and strength? Have you secured the peace of heart and mind that is an invaluable asset in life? Deciding what we lack is the first step in securing it. Christ can fulfill our needs — needs that are to some extent physical, but, more so, the deepest needs of heart and mind and soul.

"They Proclaimed It"

So often people are indifferent to the source of their blessings. Gratitude that is clearly expressed is not too prevalent. But this unbelieving man and his friends, when Christ overcame the limitations of ear and tongue, went everywhere, proclaiming the power and glory of Christ.

Another man of this same mind was J. S. Bach. He became known worldwide for his remarkable musical talent, but he never ceased to credit his Creator as the one who was responsible for his ability. The pages of his musical compositions could well have been used to satisfy a personal pride as his name appeared on them. But he was determined to give glory to God for his accomplishments. So he always concluded his original compositions with the three letters INS. They stood for the Latin words meaning "In the name of Christ." At other times Bach began his score with the letters JJ, meaning "Jesus help," and then ended his composition with the letters SDG for the Latin *Solo Deo Gloria*, meaning "To God be the glory."

We are the recipients of so much that comes to us from God. Do we "proclaim" that fact and turn acclaim away from ourselves to God?

Miracle Ten

Healing A Blind Beggar

They came to Jericho. As he and his disciples and a large crowd were leaving Jericho, Bartimaeus son of Timaeus, a blind beggar, was sitting by the roadside. When he heard that it was Jesus of Nazareth, he began to shout out and say, "Jesus, Son of David, have mercy on me!" Many sternly ordered him to be quiet, but he cried out even more loudly, "Son of David, have mercy on me!" Jesus stood still and said, "Call him here." And they called the blind man, saying to him, "Take heart; get up, he is calling you." So throwing off his cloak, he sprang up and came to Jesus. Then Jesus said to him, "What do you want me to do for you?" The blind man said to him, "My teacher, let me see again." Jesus said to him, "Go; your faith has made you well." Immediately he regained his sight and followed him on the way.

Background Material

This is the last miracle which Mark records. It concludes Mark's thrilling reports of the wondrous blessing which Christ bestowed upon the blind, the sick, the deaf, and even the dead. This particular miracle was reported by other Evangelists, who do not name the beggar. It is Mark alone who furnishes the name of Bartimaeus, which means son of Timaeus. It is somewhat curious how Mark had this information. Did he ask the man's name at the time of the miracle? Was the man a familiar beggar at this spot and thus generally known?

Although he was blind and could not see, he could hear a crowd coming along the road. The trampling feet and the conversations of the approaching group caught his attention. Out of curiosity he asked those around him to explain who was causing this commotion. To his surprise he was told that it was Jesus of Nazareth.

Jesus happened to be traveling this way, headed for Jerusalem. This miracle would mark the end of his public ministry. Just ahead lay a triumphant entry into Jerusalem, followed by a horrible crucifixion just a few days later. But after suffering death on a cross there would be the greatest miracle ever recorded: Christ's own resurrection. Before long he was to return to the Father in Heaven.

By now the fame of Jesus and the stories of his miracles had become widespread. So when he learned of the presence of Christ, a great hope surged up in the heart of the beggar. So he cried out, hoping Christ would hear him. When he was told to be quiet he disregarded the admonition and continued all the louder. His cries caught the ear of Christ, who must have sensed a need of healing. So Jesus stopped and ordered that Bartimaeus be brought to him. When they were together, though he knew what Bartimaeus wanted, Christ asked the blind man to state his desire. Was this request meant to crowd out all other thoughts in order to center on the one thing the man most wanted? Perhaps it was to rally his faith and strengthen his hope in receiving a miracle. The question is somewhat surprising since the man's need was evident and it was apparent that he had supreme confidence in Jesus to restore his sight. Surprisingly, when the miracle was performed, Jesus did not touch the man or use any elements such as clay to restore sight. Jesus simply said to Bartimaeus, "Go your way; your faith has made you whole."

Once again, Jesus is stressing the vital need of faith, not only to have one's sins forgiven and to receive the assurances of eternal life, but also to have an earthly desire fulfilled.

Jesus put no price on his miraculous healing. He did not ask the man to become one of his followers. In fact, he actually suggested another course for the man to follow, saying "Go thy way." But Bartimaeus was so filled with joy and gratitude that he happily joined the crowd around Jesus and followed him into Jerusalem. There have been conjectures about Bartimaeus and his actions during the climactic days of Christ's life. But we are left only with the knowledge that at this point he followed Christ "on the way."

Sermon Material

When Jesus Passes By

We are not living in the day when Jesus was to be seen physically on earth. We cannot call out to him when he passes near to us. But there are many ways in which Jesus crosses our lives each day. For the religiously involved there are worship services, where his presence is felt. Did he not say that where two or three are gathered in his name, he is there? Sometimes Jesus confronts us in a person who is in need, and we are able to meet that need. Christ gave us an impelling reason to visit the sick, the imprisoned, the widows, and the fatherless when he said that in doing so we are doing it to him. So we have many opportunities to draw near to Christ and to realize that he is very close by. The big questions are: How do we react? How do we take advantage of the opportunity to call out to Christ and seek his healing power? Christ is more than willing to come into our lives and meet our needs, but we should initiate the opportunity.

Instead of ignoring the passing Christ, we can call out to him and then respond to his invitation. With his presence and power we can do the good works which define those who claim to be people of faith. We can call the attention of others to the Christ who stands waiting to forgive their sins, to console, to inspire.

Persistence In Our Requests Of God

When Bartimaeus learned that Christ was passing by and called out to him for mercy, he was told by several people to be quiet. But he refused. He continued to call out to Christ all the louder and harder. In the end, Jesus heard him and asked him to come over to him. There he was told of the blindness of Bartimaeus, who asked Christ to restore his sight. Persistence is a characteristic of a strong faith. Jesus tells of a man who was visited late at night by a neighbor who was asking a favor. The request was refused until the persistence of the asker is met in order to stop the repeated request. Jesus told the parable in order to encourage us to persist when approaching God with our requests. On another occasion Jesus tells of a judge who would not answer the pleas of a widow until she had worn him down with her requests. Seeking God's help is not a one-time matter, for we must be persistent in approaching the Almighty with our requests.

Answering Christ's Invitation

When Jesus asked that Bartimaeus join him, Bartimaeus responded immediately. Note that Jesus did not go over to where the blind Bartimaeus was calling out to him. Bartimaeus had to make the move, he had to respond to Christ's invitation to come to him. A miracle was the result; he was given his sight. Jesus says to everyone, "Come unto me," and we must respond. But do we do so? Church bells announce that it is Sunday and services of worship are available. It is a day to go to church to meet Jesus, who said, "Where two or three are gathered in my name," there he is in their midst. He calls us to daily prayer. Do we respond? When tempted to do wrong do we hear his voice speaking to our conscience, or our better self? The initiative is up to us. Christ wants us to come to him with all of our life's hopes and dreams, disappointments and sorrows. Answer his bid to "come unto me."

Expressing Gratitude To God

Because he was given his sight, Bartimaeus "followed Christ." It was his way of showing gratitude for the restoration of his sight. He could have accepted the wonderful healing and then gone on his own way. Rather he became a faithful follower of Christ. Jesus reminded us of the importance of expressing gratitude when he healed the ten lepers and only one returned to give thanks for being cured from a horrible disease. We ask many things of God and do so rather frequently. Are we quick to express gratitude when our prayers are answered? Do we remember daily that God is the giver of every good and perfect gift, and then take the trouble to express our gratitude? It is a very selfish person who is glad to receive but can't be bothered to give thanks. Ann Landers is often asked what one should do who sends a gift to someone, say a grandchild, but never receives an acknowledgment or a word of thanks. This can very irritating. But ask yourself, "Since I receive so much each day from God, am I quick to say 'thank you' to him?" Ann's advice is to stop giving until a gift is acknowledged, or better still, to send an unsigned check which forces the receiver to reply in order to complete the action. We should be thankful that God does not stop giving in spite of ingratitude. So, rather than self-righteously condemning ingratitude, make sure that you are one who is always prompt in expressing gratitude.

"A Blind Beggar ... Was Sitting By The Roadside"

There are still beggars on the street in our age, mostly in large cities. We can only wonder at their story and their real need. Some are no doubt homeless. Some are badly crippled, while others could probably get a job and support themselves if they wanted to.

As we pass them, various thoughts are apt to race through our minds. We question their sincerity, and we do not wish to be gullible. Are they really crippled? Do they seek money in order to buy alcohol or drugs rather than food? Sometimes they do not make health or bodily needs an issue. Instead they say they are on their way home but are stranded without the necessary funds to buy a bus ticket or to secure a night's lodging.

Should we help them? Are they merely trying to deceive us so they can take advantage of us? When such questions confront us, we can assume one of several attitudes. We can shake them off with any one of a dozen explanations: we have no money with us, we just helped someone else and our funds are depleted. But we can also try the alternative of actually helping them. Sometimes this results in giving them money. And sometimes, wary of their statements, we go with them to a restaurant where we pay the bill and know they are spending it on food. Of course, there is always the alternative of shelling out some money in answer to their pleas for help. What should we do?

Perhaps the best plan is to help them. After all, they may truly be in need. If they are not it is they, not we, who can be criticized and have it on their conscience while ours is free of guilt or judgment of our action.

Illustrations

It Is Spring And I Am Blind

When we consider the handicap of blindness, a spring of pity arises for those who cannot see. One thinks of the beauty of nature, climaxing in a gorgeous sunrise or sunset. Then there is a full moon, or a starry night, the subjects of so many romantic songs. A blind person is denied the joy of seeing the faces of loved ones, including little children.

An impressive story of a blind man is one that tells of a man on the streets of New York City. It was in the beautiful month of May and people were enjoying a spring morning. Their emotions were stirred when they came upon this blind beggar who carried a sign reading: "It is spring and I am blind." He knew that there was beauty all around him: spring flowers, blossoming shrubs and trees, newly-sprouted little leaves, but he could only imagine how wonderful all that beauty was. It must be vexing to smell spring in the air but not be able to witness this wonderful time of year.

Do we fully appreciate the blessings of sight which God has given us? Are we moved to express gratitude for so wonderful a physical sense?

Second Sight

A line in a hymn reads, "I was blind, but now I see." It is not referring to physical blindness, but to a lack of vision of the spiritual world. There is a spiritual blindness which can be a great handicap to the health of our soul. It is possible to see physically, but not to do so spiritually. We can have our vision, yet not see that we are sinners in need of a Savior. We can view our earthly possessions, but be blinded to the fact that we have not laid up any treasure in heaven. Just as Christ healed Bartimaeus of physical blindness, he can lead us to comprehend our spiritual state. We have heard people use the phrase, "I see, said the blind man." It is not a contradiction, but refers to the insight beyond our physical situation. Have you received your second sight?

Jesus Passes By

Little Selby was drawing a picture with pen and ink. It turned out to be a cat without a tail. "Where's the tail?" asked her mother. Selby looked puzzled for a moment and then replied, "Why, it's in the ink bottle yet."

So many of the good things we plan to do are like that; they are still in the ink bottle. They are an intention that has not been carried out. This can be true of the greatest thing in life: the will to follow Christ and live out our life as belonging to him. He is now near at hand, as he was to the blind Bartimaeus. But we have to realize that now is the time to put into action our good intentions about Christ. It was the English essayist Joseph Addison who said: "We are always complaining that our days are few, and acting as if there were no end of them."

* * *

The blind Bartimaeus did not let the opportunity slip away to reach out to Jesus as he passed by. As a result he became a follower of the Lord and could lead a fulfilled life. All about us are people who do not realize that it is the lack of Christ in their lives which can account for their failures. We have learned something important about suicides as a result of serious study. Suicides are not most frequent among the poor and destitute, as we might expect. They occur among the people who have so much of the good things of life. It has become evident that those who commit suicide may have much in the way of worldly goods, but they lack something to live for. They have not developed a desire for the life that is more than meat.

Meeting Christ

History tells some stories about a few times when two people met each other dramatically to discuss matters which carried serious consequences. This occurred on July 25, 1807, at a spot in the Tilsit River in Prussia. In the middle of that stream Napoleon and Alexander held a much publicized private conference. It was widely described in advance as a meeting which would "arrange the destinies of humankind." Cannons boomed, and the shouts of thousands of soldiers gathered on each side of the river added to the noise as the conference began.

Bartimaeus had an opportunity to meet Christ, one on one, and took advantage of it. As a result, he was greatly blessed. You and I have the same privilege of meeting with Christ, one on one. Christ is calling to us, saying, "Come unto me." Such an encounter, for each one of us, is by far the most important in our lives, for it determines our eternal destiny.

Persistence

Those around him tried to hush Bartimaeus as he was calling out to Christ. But he persisted. When Christ called him as a result of his persistent crying out, he was healed of his blindness.

The story is told of a man being chased by a lion while on an African safari. The man saw a tree a short distance ahead, with a branch crossing his path a little above his head. When he reached the branch he made a mighty leap. When telling the story later he was asked, "Did you manage to reach up to the branch?" "No," the man replied, "but I caught it on the way down."

Often it is on the second or third try that one succeeds in gaining what one seeks. Persistence helps. We must be willing to repeat our prayer requests.

Jesus Said, "Call Him"

During World War II, after a German attack, an American boy returned to his company after a sick leave and discovered that his army buddy, with whom he had fought side by side, was being reported as missing in action. Immediately he asked permission to go back over the battlefield in search of his friend. His officer strongly advised him not to go on such an errand, saying, "If you go, it will not be worth it. Go at your own risk, but I am sure it will cost you your life." The young soldier went out, found his friend badly hurt, and carried him back to his own line. But at this point the wounded man died. Then the rescuer himself was shot. The officer, leaning over the rescuer just before he died, said, "I told you that you would lose your life if you ventured out on the battlefield. Was it worth it?" "Yes, sir," the dying man replied. "When my friend saw me he said, 'I knew you would come.'"

* * *

Christ is counting on you to come in answer to his call. To you, Christ is saying, "Come unto me." If you do not have a great deal of courage to be a Christian, no matter what, you will wilt before this challenge. If your heart is not filled with Christian love you will not heed the call to serve him. Christ confronts you with this challenge. Do with it what you will. "Come unto me."

Meeting Human Needs By Ways Other Than With Money

A man was walking along the street of a big city when he was accosted by a beggar. Deciding to help the beggar, the man stopped and reached into his pocket for his wallet. The action encouraged the beggar, who waited expectantly. But then the man realized that in leaving home he had inadvertently forgotten to pick up his wallet and so had no means of giving a gift. "Friend," he said to the beggar, "I'm sorry but I forgot and left my wallet at home. I'm sorry, but I can't help you."

"That's all right," answered the beggar. "You have already given me a big lift. You called me friend."

Epilogue

The miracles of Christ present a joyful opportunity for pastors in their sermon preparation. If one immerses oneself in the biblical accounts of Christ's miracle-working ministry, one receives a spiritual uplift which is not available elsewhere. It is a privilege to tell others of the miraculous powers of our Lord. There is pure joy in the telling. They provide a wide variety of sermon subjects. When one preaches with spirit on these acts of Christ, the congregation is both absorbed and enlightened. And the task of sermon preparation is made easier.

This material is not intended to present a complete sermon, but rather to serve as a thought-starter, a basis on which the pastor's own thoughts can emerge. It should prove to be a considerable help to anyone engaged in such service.

We should not make the mistake of thinking that only a few disciples, like John Mark or other New Testament individuals, believed in the mysterious powers of God performing miracles on earth through Christ. It is well to remember that, beginning with Moses, biblical writers give assurances of the miracles of God. An example would be the host of miracles occurring in the process of bringing God's people out from under their oppressive Egyptian rulers. The recitation of the plagues is a wonderful prologue to the miracles of God in the New Testament. The affirmation of miracles in the Old Testament continues with Daniel in the lions' den and the trial in the fiery furnace of Meshach, Shadrach, and Abednego. Far from being a singular repertoire of miracles, the Gospel writers are confirmed by numerous accounts of such incidents in both the Old and the New Testaments.

Mark's emphasis on the miracles of Christ is to picture Jesus as a man of divine power. His purpose in writing was to encourage his readers to see that Christ could have performed his miracles only if he were the Son of God. There is really no other explanation for the people flocking to Christ in such numbers, drawn by his spreading reputation as a miracle worker. In addition to the vast crowds of common people who surged around Christ, even some in palaces became interested in him. No less a figure than Herod heard of the works of Christ and apparently believed in them, though not enough to accept Christ as a Messiah because that was, in his judgment, a religious teaching of the Jews.

It should be reiterated that the material contained here is not intended to present a complete sermon, but rather to supply material that will inspire the pastor to add his thoughts in preparing a sermon. It should prove to be a big help to anyone charged with this responsibility.

Occasionally we might ask ourselves why we do certain things the way we do. One answer would be the persuasive power of advertising on television and in magazines and newspapers, or even the nudging of friends. But what is it that leads us to Christ, to become people of faith, determined to follow him? The crowds drawn to Christ during his earthly ministry sometimes came to witness a miracle worker performing his acts. Others came to Christ to secure something from him: a healing, or the return from death of a loved one. Such reasons are both selfish and materialistic. So why else should one be drawn to Jesus? John Mark wanted us to do so for spiritual health and healing. Christ can enter into our life and make us whole, causing us to live by faith and not by bread alone.

So many questions can arise naturally in one's mind, questions that demand answers in order to soothe our restless souls. Those questions are these: "Who am I? Why am I here? What purpose is there in my life? What does death bring to me?" There are many others. All such questions are answered satisfactorily in the teachings and example of Christ. Mark tries to show us that we need to come to Christ to find the deepest answers to those questions. Scripture describes the desire to have Christ in our life as a hungering and thirsting after righteousness. There is a need for Christ in one's life in order to build a healthy life on a sane basis and thus find our own fulfillment.

While one purpose of Christ's life was to reveal to Jews the fulfillment of their own prophecies and teachings, he stressed universality. He broke the bonds and limitations of Judaism.

Salvation is for all who repent. He clearly stated that whosoever believed in him would have eternal life. He selected a number of Jewish laws to give them proper perspective, making them a part of Christian teaching. His phrasing was, "You have heard it said ... But I say unto you."

Worthy of mention is the fact that all of Christ's miracles were positive, they were productive of good, they involved healing and even life after death. Though they could have been, they were never used defensively or in retribution. There were times when they could have been so used, as in the Garden of Gethsemane when his enemies came to take him by force or when his enemies were mocking him. But instead, his miracles were always productive of blessings on others.

As for miracles in modern life, we must realize that while it may be good to request them of God, we must follow Christ's example of resignation to the divine will. ("Not my will but thine be done.") Though we may not realize it at the time, sometimes there is too much good that comes from a situation for it to be changed immediately. Sickness, for instance, can chasten the proud and turn one's thoughts away from the emphasis on earthly considerations. Like grapes that must be crushed to make wine, the human spirit must sometimes be subjected to pain and denial in order to mature. When our prayers for a miracle are not answered, we should not become critical or yield to despair. We are still in the hands of God, who knows what is best for us and loves us. He grieves when we suffer, and he knows what we endure. As we know, God will sometimes not answer a prayer for healing. Then we must believe that suffering is a means of strengthening our faith, as we increasingly rely upon God to help us through a time of trial. Sometimes we even have to wait patiently until we receive our perfect bodies in heaven. The conclusion of the matter is this: believe in miracles, but trust God's wisdom and have faith.

Bibliography

The Interpreter's Bible, Volume 7. New York: Abingdon Cokesbury Press, 1951.

Brokhoff, John. *Preaching The Miracles, Cycle B*. Lima, Ohio: CSS Publishing Company, 1990.

Evely, Louis. (J. F. Bernard, Translator). *The Gospels Without Myth*. New York: Doubleday, 1971.

Kee, Howard Clark. *The Origins of Christianity*. Englewood Cliffs, New Jersey: Prentice-Hall, 1973.

Laymon, Charles M., ed. *The Interpreter's One Volume Commentary on the Bible*. Nashville, Tennessee: Abingdon Press, 1971.

Lockyer, Herbert. *All the Miracles of the Bible*. Grand Rapids, Michigan: Zondervan Publishing House, 1961.

Neiman, Carol. *Miracles*. New York: Viking Studio Books , 1995.

Rouner, A. A., Jr. *Master of Men*. Minneapolis, Minnesota: T. S. Denison and Company, Inc., 1966.

www.ingramcontent.com/pod-product-compliance
Lightning Source LLC
LaVergne TN
LVHW051656080426
835511LV00017B/2598